GILLY CUBITT
AND JUDY WIL

CHILDREN'S
PARTIES

HAMLYN

First published in 1986
This edition published in 1990 by
The Hamlyn Publishing Group Ltd,
a division of the Octopus Publishing Group,
Michelin House, 81 Fulham Road,
London SW3 6RB

copyright © 1986 The Hamlyn Publishing Group Ltd

Produced by New Leaf Productions

Photography by Mick Duff
Design by Jim Wire
Typeset by System Graphics Ltd, Folkestone
Edited by Josephine Bacon

ISBN 0 600 32637 3

Produced by Mandarin Offset
Printed and bound in Hong Kong

NOTE
Metric measures are not direct conversions so never
metric and imperial in a recipe.

We would like to thank:
Mum and Dad for the original inspiration, Linda W
for typing the manuscript.

Superted – copyright © Petalcraft Demonstrations Ltd
1982 & 1985

CONTENTS

INTRODUCTION

We hope this book will inspire you and give you confidence, when faced with your first children's party, or when you have had so many that you need an injection of new ideas! Children are easily inspired and love attending parties, but the organiser sometimes finds it difficult to work up the necessary enthusiasm to make it all go with a swing, and to enjoy it personally. This is where this book can help to make the day. There are 13 different themes for parties; each section includes instructions for making a cake, suitable games and how to play them, as well as recipes your children will love. None of these parties require special skills or equipment. We have suggested an age range for each party but we've assumed that children under three and over twelve do not want this kind of structured party.

THINKING AHEAD

When you're thinking of throwing a children's party there are several factors to consider in order to ensure the whole thing runs smoothly and is fun for everyone.

Consider how many children you can cope with, how long you will have to prepare food, and how much time you want to devote to organising games, before you embark on something too ambitious and time-consuming. You may need to spread the preparation over several days and choose food that can be frozen well in advance.

Some parties in this book are suited to a particular age group, but several will suit a mixed age range—especially important where there are brothers and sisters to consider.

The first thing to do is to send out interesting invitations so that the guests are intrigued and excited about coming. We've suggested ideas within the party themes that you may like to use or adapt.

Decide whether you want the children to dress up and if you yourself are prepared to dress up. If it's an indoors-outdoors party, suggest old clothes and sensible shoes.

To a certain extent, some foods are more suitable for certain types of party. For instance you won't want to transport a gooey chocolate cake or meringues to a picnic party. We've taken this into account when menu-planning, but of course you can mix and match recipes from any of the parties.

We've suggested ways in which to create a party atmosphere, using appropriate props and music where necessary. The games are adapted slightly to suit the theme of the party but many are games that the children will know. There may be some that *you* don't know and may have fun playing for the first time!

Consider, too, whether you plan to give prizes. It can cause friction among younger children, but older children like to be competitive. In a game like Pass the Parcel, a small gift or packet of sweets may be included between each layer—but then the organiser has to make sure that each child gets one. Other games, say Musical Statues, can end with a round of applause for the winner, and a sweet or small gift for everyone.

Don't make the party too long. It is much better if it finishes while everyone is enjoying themselves and before the children reach the arguing stage. Two and a half hours is a good length 'do', as this allows enough time to unwrap the presents, play games, eat tea and play a few more games before it is time to go.

A lot of parties end up with the distribution of goody bags for the children to take away. These, if you wish to include them, need not contain expensive gifts but tokens such as a balloon, a piece of cake and a few sweets. If the children have made or won anything at the party they can add that to it.

PLANNING THE PARTY

If at all possible, enlist some adult assistance, even if it's just to help pour drinks, do a bit of washing up, and help out if anything unexpected happens.

Have a list of games ready and decide in which order you will play them. It is worth remembering that games seldom last as long as you think, so have an activity lined up for the end of the party. This could be just paper and crayons for drawing, or decorating paper hats made in advance. If you are feeling energetic the day before, dye some fancy-shaped noodles with food colouring and mix them up with cut lengths of drinking straws. Supply some fine string so the children can thread up a necklace to take home.

Present-opening can be a tricky time. The birthday boy or girl is given a lot of presents to open all at once, so they tend to rush through them, distracted by quantity rather than quality. Some parents prefer to keep presents to be opened after the party. If you choose to do this, keep a note of who gave what so you can help your child to write a thank-you letter. This can work well if you have lots of guests, but the givers may be disappointed. Help your child appreciate the gifts he receives.

Some children, especially the little ones, find it hard to leave their mum or dad and enter the hurly-burly of a party. If a child does get upset ask his parents to stay until he or she has calmed down, or let the parent remain for the duration if necessary. Otherwise, the poor child will not settle and you'll find yourself nursing a tearful child, organising Pass the Parcel and trying to dish up the hot dogs, all at the same time!

Check beforehand that none of the children are on special diets. If possible, make something similar to the rest of the food for them, or if it's tricky, ask their parents to supply you with the right food. A handicapped child among the guests may need extra help from an adult, so make plans accordingly.

For safety's sake, shut outside doors and gates when young children are about. If the children are allowed free range of the house put anything precious away or out of reach. Tell the children that rooms with closed doors are out of bounds. Make space by re-arranging the furniture. If you have an excitable dog, ask someone to take it for a long walk for the duration of the party.

Decorating the house always adds to the party spirit, and if you can do this while the child is out, perhaps at school, it makes a wonderful surprise for them to come home to. Balloons tied to the door show the children where to come. Birthday cards on a string along the walls, noisy music and the birthday cake displayed for all to see are little touches that get the party off to a grand start, and set the atmosphere for the rest to come.

Ask a helper to take some photographs for you as you may not get the opportunity.

One thing you can't control is the weather! Summer-born children will probably have some, if not all, of their party in the garden. But it may rain, so be prepared with alternative activities or games that can be played in or out of doors. It can be an enormous advantage to have a mixed age range with older children to help the smaller ones with the games. Young children like older ones around and it makes group games much easier to set up and run.

It is important for the organisers to be enthusiastic and get totally involved. The party won't last long, so give it your all. Have something for the helpers to eat and drink so everyone enjoys the party!

ALL-IN-ONE CAKE

A good, reliable, basic cake mix made in minutes and suitable for many different finishes.

SIZE ONE
100 g/4 oz soft margarine
100 g/4 oz caster sugar
2 eggs
100 g/4 oz self raising flour
1 teaspoon baking powder

SIZE TWO
175 g/6 oz soft margarine
175 g/6 oz caster sugar
3 eggs
175 g/6 oz self raising flour
1½ teaspoons baking powder

SIZE THREE
225 g/8 oz soft margarine
225 g/8 oz caster sugar
4 eggs
225 g/8 oz self raising flour
2 teaspoons baking powder

All sizes are made in the same way – just put all the ingredients in a bowl (or mixer) and beat well for two minutes. Grease and line the base of the baking tin with greaseproof paper. Bake in a moderate oven (180°C, 350°F, gas 4). The cooking times vary according to the size and shape of the tins which is shown with the cooking times and decorating instructions for each cake recipe.

Variations
Lemon and Orange
Add the grated rind of 1 lemon or orange to the mixture.

Chocolate
Replace 1-3 tablespoons of flour with the same quantity of cocoa powder.

BUTTER ICING

100 g/4 oz butter
225 g/8 oz icing sugar, sifted
flavouring (optional)

Beat the butter until softened. Gradually beat in the icing sugar, and any flavouring.

Flavourings
1–2 tablespoons lemon or orange juice
1 teaspoon instant coffee, dissolved in 1
 teaspoon hot water
1 tablespoon cocoa replacing 1 tablespoon icing
 sugar

To apply butter icing

Soften 4 tablespoonfuls of the icing with 1 teaspoon warm water. Spread it over the cakes in a thin layer; it will spread easily, without detaching crumbs. Once the cake is thinly coated, it's easier to spread or pipe the rest of the stiffer butter icing on top.

DECORATION ICING

1 egg white
1 rounded tablespoon liquid glucose
450 g/1 lb icing sugar
cornflour

Mix the egg white and liquid glucose together. Gradually mix in the sifted icing sugar until it is too stiff to stir. Knead in the remaining icing sugar to give a smooth, elastic consistency.

To apply decoration icing

Decoration icing sets hard when exposed to air, so it's essential to keep it tightly wrapped until you are ready to use it. First spread the cake thinly with warmed apricot jam. (Jam can be warmed in the pot, by standing it in a bowl of hot water). Dust a working surface with icing sugar and roll out the icing to the right size. Keep lifting it to check that it's not sticking. Lift carefully onto the rolling pin and drape the icing over the cake. Using fingertips dusted with cornflour stretch and smooth the icing into position and neaten the corners. Trim off any excess. Dust off the cornflour with a dry pastry brush. Paint the icing with food colourings and add other decorations.

FOOD COLOURINGS

Liquid food colourings, available in dropper bottles, are suitable for many colouring jobs. However they tend to produce pale colours and are too diluted for painting directly onto decoration icing. Paste or gel colourings, available from cookshops and special cake decorating suppliers, are more expensive but can give much stronger colours. Apply them with a damp paint brush when painting directly onto decoration icing. Or, beat or knead a little paste or gel colouring directly into icing. Remember that the colours tend to intensify as the icing dries.

PIRATE PARTY

This is a party that requires a fair bit of pre-planning and preparation but the children will get immense enjoyment out of it, so it really is well worth the effort. Once again, the invitations can spark off initial enthusiasm, especially if you take the time to make them from greaseproof paper, roughly torn, and scorched at the edges on an electric ring or gas burner. This is definitely a job for an adult but the writing and addition of a splodge of red food colouring in the corner to suggest blood is a job a child will love to tackle.

It is a huge advantage if the weather is on your side, so you can use the garden. Turn a climbing frame, swing, or picnic bench into a pirate ship, fly a flag from the top and add an old sheet for the sail. But even indoors, you can make use of whatever furniture is around, whether it be old armchairs, under the kitchen table, or even the bunk beds. Children have wonderful imaginations and only need a few basics to set the scene and create the right atmosphere.

When the children arrive they should be invited to sign the log book. They will then be issued with an eye patch (made from a piece of black card cut to the right shape and threaded on fine elastic) and a headscarf, or scrap of material to tie round the head in true pirate fashion. If the parents dress up as well and surprise the children the party becomes more exciting. This only requires some scruffy clothes, a belt, cardboard swords and a scar painted on the cheek!

The food is designed for eating with the fingers like any self-respecting pirate. You'll need plenty of paper napkins. A treasure island cake with a small gift buried inside for the lucky winner makes a grand finale.

The games suggested here can all be adapted slightly to suit the children invited to the party. A mixed age range is useful as the older ones can help, lead groups, and read out instructions.

TREASURE HUNT

This is a game where each group needs a leader who can read. You'll need to write and hide clues before the party. Give each group their first clue which will lead to the second, third and eventually the treasure! Clues could be written on singed greaseproof again, or use chalk marks and pointers. There should be different clues for each group so they can find their own treasure, instead of all racing for the same spot.

Chocolate coins wrapped in gold foil make excellent edible treasures, real coins in small denominations can seem like a fortune to children and will last (a little) longer.

PASS THE PARROT

This game is simply a variation of Pass the Parcel but the package should be shaped and painted in bright colours to look like a parrot. A small prize in each layer helps maintain enthusiasm, but make sure there are enough for them to get one each before the final prize is reached. The children sit in a circle, passing the parcel, while music plays. When the music stops the person holding the parcel takes off just one layer of paper. When the music starts again, the parcel is passed on. This continues until the lucky winner removes the last layer and keeps the gift inside.

APPLE BOBBING

This is a game for slightly older children who don't mind getting their faces wet. A bowl or bath filled with water has either small whole, or half apples floating in it. The child has to get the apple out using only mouths and teeth, not hands. A variation on the theme is to attempt to eat ring doughnuts tied onto pieces of string suspended from the washing line!

JUMP THE RIVER

Put two pieces of rope or garden canes, about 2-metres/6-feet apart on the ground. While the music is playing, the children have to leap or run from one side to the other. when the music stops all the children caught in the 'river' are out.

TREASURE ISLAND

**1 28 × 18 × 4-cm/11 × 7 × 1½-inch cake, use
   size two cake mix (see page 6)**
tiny gift
1 quantity butter icing
½ quantity decoration icing
orange, blue, green and brown food colourings
candles and candleholders

Bake the cake for 25–30 minutes. Put the cake onto a
board. Push a tiny gift wrapped in cling film inside
the cake. Colour the butter icing blue and spread it
over the sides and top of the cake. Colour half the
decoration icing orange. Make two small sausage
shapes with icing and place them on the cake to make
mountains. Roll out a roughly oval-shaped island
and position it on the butter icing, over the mountain
shapes. Make a blue butter icing lagoon in the centre.
Using the remaining icing, model trees and ship-
wrecks and place them on the island or in the sea.
Paint with green and brown food colouring. Add
candles in holders.

CROSS-BONES
Serves 12

We've let you off the skulls but cross-bones are a
must at a pirate feast!

12 chicken drumsticks
4 tablespoons honey
2 tablespoons vinegar
4 tablespoons soy-sauce

Prick the drumsticks in several places with a fork.
Brush a roasting tin lightly with oil. Arrange
drumsticks in the tin. Mix the honey, vinegar and
soy-sauce together and brush liberally over the
chicken. Cook in a moderately hot oven (190°C,
375°F, gas 5) for about 30 minutes until the juices run
clear when meat is pierced with a fine skewer. Serve
hot or cold.

SAUSAGE CHAINS
Serves 12

Supply kitchen scissors for the children to cut themselves a 'link' and cocktail sticks to spear the sausages with.

675 g/1½ lb pork or beef chipolatas, linked

Leave the sausages linked together and twist each one in the middle, to make two sausages out of one. Put the strings in a greased roasting tin and cook in a moderately hot oven (200°C, 400°F, gas 6) for about 30 minutes, turning sausages carefully halfway through cooking time. Drain on kitchen paper then transfer to a serving dish.

GOLDEN NUGGETS
Makes 24

225 g/8 oz flour
good pinch salt
2 eggs, separated
300 ml/½ pint milk
350 g/12 oz frozen sweetcorn, cooked
oil for deep frying

Sift the flour and salt into a bowl, make a well in the centre and add the egg yolks. Mix together gently with half the milk to make a smooth paste. Beat in the rest of the milk. Just before cooking, add the cooked sweetcorn to the batter. Whisk the egg whites until stiff but not dry and fold carefully into the batter. Heat the oil in a deep frying pan to 180°C, 350°F. Fry a few spoonfuls of the mixture at a time for 3–4 minutes, turning once, until crisp and brown. Drain on kitchen paper. Reheat, if necessary, uncovered, in a moderate oven (180°C, 350°F, gas 4) for 10–15 minutes before serving.

'MOULDY BREAD'
Serves 12

Everybody knows what a poor diet pirates have and 'mouldy' bread is a vital part of it!

Large French stick
225 g/8 oz crunchy peanut butter

Cut the French stick in half if necessary to fit in your oven, but cut it diagonally. Cut 12 diagonal slices almost through the bread every 2-cm/¾-inch or so. Spread the inside of each slit thickly with peanut butter. Put the two halves side by side on a baking tray and cook in a moderately hot oven (190°C, 375°F, gas 5) for about 20 minutes until crisp and brown. Separate the slices using kitchen scissors and serve warm.

SHIP'S BISCUITS
Makes 36

These biscuits are best eaten fresh before the cornflakes lose their crispness.

175 g/6 oz soft margarine
175 g/6 oz caster sugar
1 egg, beaten
few drops vanilla essence
225 g/8 oz self-raising flour
handful of cornflakes, to coat

Cream the margarine and sugar in a bowl until light and fluffy. Beat in the egg, vanilla essence and flour to form a soft dough. Spread the cornflakes on a plate and roll spoonfuls of the biscuit mixture in them. Place on greased baking trays leaving space between them. Flatten slightly and cook in a moderate oven (180°C, 350°F, gas 4) for 20 minutes or until pale golden-brown. Allow to cool slightly on trays, before transferring to a wire rack to finish cooling.

CANNONBALLS
Makes 24

350 g/12 oz chocolate cake crumbs
225 g/8 oz chocolate and hazelnut spread

Crumble the cake into a bowl. Add the chocolate and hazelnut spread and gradually mash the crumbs into it, using a fork. Roll tablespoonfuls of the mixture into smooth balls with your hands. Coat them with vermicelli and leave to set in a cool place.

SUPERTED PARTY

We suggest an age range of five to ten for this party as these children are his greatest fans. A wide range of Superted disposable paperware is available so you could carry the theme right through the party with no washing-up afterwards.

Use it too, to decorate the house. Pin tablecloths on the wall, hang Superted balloons and give Superted pencils, pads or the miniature Teds as prizes.

Even the invitations can be teddy-shaped. Fold an oblong of paper 23 × 7.5-cm/9 × 3-inch into five equal parts like you would a fan. Draw a teddy on the front and cut him out leaving his hands and feet joined. When you unfold the paper you will have five bears for colouring and writing the details of the party. Leave the last teddy blank, putting dotted lines where he joined teddy number four. The recipient will then know to cut this one off and send back his or her answer. (If you have a teddy cutter for biscuits you could draw round it.)

See also our Superted-inspired recipes and cake.

SQUEAK SUPERTED SQUEAK

All the children except one sit down around the room. The child in the middle is blindfolded and given a small cushion. The rest of the children swap places, then the 'seeker' must feel his way around until he finds a lap to sit on. He or she puts the cushion on first, sits on it and says 'Squeak Superted Squeak'. The squashed (and by now giggling) person has to squeak and the squasher has to guess who he or she is. If he or she guesses correctly, a cheer goes up and someone else has a turn at being blindfolded.

SPOTTYMAN HAS MEASLES

Before your child disappears for the day, make him or her lie down on a piece of wallpaper and draw round them. This gives you the shape on which to draw Spottyman. Make spots out of sticky green paper. Hang Spottyman on the wall and hide all the spots around the house. Make sure there is nothing fragile in places they are likely to look and that doors of out-of-bounds rooms are closed. When a child finds a spot he must write his name of the front and stick the spot onto Spottyman. As your children will know, when Spottyman has measles all his spots disappear, so as they find his spots they are helping him to recover. The child who finds the most spots is the winner.

TEX'S FOOTSTEPS

You will need a bit of space for this game. One child stands out in front as far away as possible from the others and with his or her back to them. He or she is "Tex". The children have to creep up on Tex (who can be wearing a cowboy hat if you have one). He or she turns round frequently to catch the other children moving. If Tex sees anyone moving that person must go back to the start. The child that reaches Tex and touches him or her first then becomes Tex.

PUT BONES TOGETHER

For this game you will need to employ some of your latent artistic skill. Draw the bones of the body, the skull, neckbone, backbone, pelvis, four bones for the arms and four larger, but similar bones for the legs, plus blue gloves and red shoes. (Refer to a picture of Skeleton to get the right idea). There are several ways you could play the game. Let each child assemble the bits, timing them. Or divide into teams, each with a set of bones and roll a dice awarding the skull for a six, the arms and legs for fours etc. Or get the children to earn the different pieces with a forfeit such as doing a somersault, singing a song or eating two dry crackers in less than one minute. The first team to complete a whole skeleton is the winner.

SPOTTY'S COOKIES
Makes 24

75 g/3 oz butter
175 g/6 oz soft brown sugar
1 egg
75 g/3 oz self-raising flour
75 g/3 oz wholewheat flour
100 g/4 oz chocolate dots

Cream butter and sugar until light and fluffy, then beat in the egg. Fold in the flours and chocolate dots. Put spoonfuls of the mixture onto greased baking trays, allowing room for spreading. Bake in a moderate oven (180°C, 350°F, gas 4) for 12–15 minutes. Allow to cool on trays for 2–3 minutes, then transfer to a wire rack to cool completely.

SOARAWAY SUPERTED

1 20-cm/8-inch round cake, use size two cake
   mix (see page 6)
1 18-cm/7-inch round cake, use size one cake
   mix (see page 6)
1 quantity butter icing
½ quantity decoration icing
assorted food colourings

Bake the cake for 30–35 minutes and the smaller cake for 25–30 minutes. Put the larger cake on a large board. Cut the projecting shapes of Superted's head and arms out from the smaller cake. Use some butter icing or jam to stick them next to the main cake. Roll out three-quarters of the decoration icing and cut out the shapes for Superted's head, limbs and body. Assemble him on the cake. Coat the sides of the cake with plain butter icing. Colour the remaining butter icing green. Spread it on top of cake, around Superted. Colour the remaining decoration icing yellow and roll it out. Use a 2.5-cm/1-inch cutter to cut out spots. Arrange them on the 'planet' behind Superted. Using the appropriate colours, paint Superted's features and costume.

SPOTTY SAUSAGE PIZZAS
Makes 12

6 soft hamburger buns
8 tablespoons tomato relish
175 g/6 oz grated cheese
2 Peperami sausages

Split buns in half and arrange on a baking tray. Spread tomato relish over and cover with grated cheese, pressing it on well. Slice Peperami sausages and dot over cheese. Cook in a moderately hot oven (190°C, 375°F, gas 5) for 20 minutes until cheese is bubbling and golden. Serve warm.

SUPERTED SANDWICHES
Makes 12

About 4 tablespoons softened butter or margarine
24 thin slices bread
soft, spreading pâté
fish paste
sandwich spread
1 small cucumber
tub of salad cress

Butter the bread thinly, but don't spread butter or filling right to the edges. Make four pâté sandwiches, four fish paste and four sandwich spread. Cut off the crusts, and cut each sandwich with a teddy-shaped biscuit cutter. Wrap sandwiches in cling film until required. Arrange on a serving dish with sticks of cucumber and salad cress.

STRIPED BLANCMANGE
Serves 12

"Bubbling Blancmange" is a famous Superted exclamation. It's good to eat too!

**3 packets blancmange in assorted flavours e.g.
  peach, strawberry and banana**
1.75 litres/3 pints milk
6 tablespoons sugar

Make up all three blancmanges, one at a time, with the milk, and sugar, according to the directions on the packet. Rinse out a 2 litre/3½ pint mould (or two smaller moulds) with cold water. Pour in the banana blancmange. Leave to set with the mould tipped slightly. Repeat with the strawberry then finally the peach blancmange. Chill until set. Loosen edge of blancmange then dip mould in hot water for 10 seconds. Turn out onto a serving plate.

BULK'S BARS
Makes 12

100 g/4 oz butter
100 g/4 oz marshmallows
100 g/4 oz toffees
100 g/4 oz Rice Krispies

Gently heat the butter, marshmallows and toffees in a saucepan until melted. Bring to the boil and boil for 1 minute. Remove from the heat and stir in the Krispies. Spread into a greased and base-lined 18 × 28-cm/7 × 11-inch Swiss roll tin. Smooth the top and leave to set. Cut into 12 bars while still slightly warm and remove from tin when cold.

PADDLING POOL PARTY

This party is most suitable for little children with summer birthdays. Youngsters below the age of three don't really appreciate organised parties as they prefer to go their own way, but if they have older brothers or sisters then this party will entertain them too. You'll need a paddling pool, baby bath, or even several washing-up bowls. Save lots of plastic bottles and cartons, any bath toys you have, dolls, dolls' clothes, anything that will be fun to play with in water. Warn the mothers in advance so the children come armed with towels and not wearing their best clothes. With children as young as this, the mums will stay, so lay on some refreshments for them. Prepare as much as possible the evening and morning before the 'do', so you can join in. Children of this young age just like nibbles rather than a full spread, so you will need crisps, cubes of cheese, tiny sausages, Krispie cakes, fruit, and perhaps ice-lollies or ice-cream, rather than sandwiches. The mums will probably like to nibble too so we've included recipes for dips with pitta bread, and crudités.

Invitations could be made from card, with pictures cut from magazines and catalogues or drawings that are relevant to children or swimming. If you are feeling artistic, draw a paddling pool with children's faces peeping over the top. They could be shouting the details of the party.

You won't be indoors much so shut internal doors to keep wet feet and soggy bottoms off the furniture. Have other toys in the garden for those who don't want to get wet or those that have finished playing with the water. You could have a sand pit, a box of cars, a basketful of interesting things for very little ones to sort through and throw around, some things to push or ride on. In fact, as many different activities as you are prepared to clear up afterwards.

CURRANT AND RAISIN PARCELS

Cut corners from small plastic sandwich bags. Fill with a few raisins, currants and banana chips if liked. Twist tie the top of the bag and give the children one each to open so they can discover the contents for themselves.

KRISPIE CAKES

100 g/4 oz chocolate-flavoured cake covering
50 g/2 oz Rice Krispies
paper petits-fours cases

Melt the cake covering in a bowl over a pan of simmering water. Stir in Krispies until evenly coated with chocolate. Put teaspoonfuls into each paper case and leave to cool and set.

PADDLING POOL CAKE

1 20-cm/8-inch diameter round cake, use size two cake mix (see page 6)
1 quantity decoration icing
blue and orange food colourings
2 tablespoons apricot jam, warmed
1 small doll
other toys (optional)
1 tablet lemon jelly

Bake the cake for 30–35 minutes. Place cake upside-down on a board. Spread jam around the side of the cake. Colour half the decoration icing blue. Roll the blue icing into three long 'sausages'. Roll two white 'sausages' in the same way. Wrap them alternately round the cake with the joins at the back. Cut a hole in the centre of the cake and sit a small doll in it. Colour a little decoration icing orange and make

armbands for the doll, plus a duck and other toys if liked. Make up the jelly with only half recommended quantity of water. When half-set, spoon it round the doll. Leave to set.

Susan

Dear Hayley,
I am having a paddling pool party for my 3rd birthday. Will you come along and help me celebrate. Bring mummy as well from 3-5pm, Thursday 15th July at 146 Sefton Avenue. Dont forget to bring your swimming things! Love Julia
RSVP

TARAMASALATA
Serves 12

5 thin slices white bread
150 ml/¼ pint water
1 small onion, chopped
150 ml/¼ pint oil
100-g/4-oz can smoked cod roe
2 tablespoons lemon juice
1 tablespoon wine vinegar

Soak the bread in the water for 10 minutes. Squeeze out bread and put into a liquidiser with the onion and oil. Blend for 30 seconds. Add remaining ingredients and blend to a smooth dip. Season to taste. Serve with pitta bread fingers.

HUMMUS
Serves 12

400-g/14-oz can chickpeas
1 clove garlic, crushed
1 small onion, chopped
2 tablespoons tahini★
6 tablespoons oil
2 to 3 teaspoons lemon juice

Purée the contents of the can of chickpeas in a liquidiser. Add the garlic, onion and tahini. Add the oil a little at a time until the mixture has the consistency of whipped cream. Add lemon juice and seasoning to taste. Serve with pitta bread fingers.

★Tahini is a paste made from sesame seeds. Jars are easily obtained in delicatessens or health food shops.

PITTA BREAD FINGERS

Allow half a pitta bread per person. Dip bread quickly into water, then grill for about 1 minute each side. Using kitchen scissors, cut into halves, then into fingers. Wrap fingers in a clean tea towel to keep them warm.

MAYONNAISE DIPS

You could always buy mayonnaise and just add the yogurt and herbs, but this is a handy recipe to have, and tastier than shop-bought mayonnaise.

2 egg yolks
½ teaspoon powdered mustard
2 tablespoons white wine vinegar
300 ml/½ pint corn or sunflower oil
1 tablespoon boiling water
4 tablespoons natural yogurt
2 tablespoons chopped parsley
1 tablespoon chopped chives or spring onion

Put the egg yolks, mustard and 1 tablespoon of the vinegar in a liquidiser and blend for a few seconds. While the machine is still running, gently trickle in half the oil, then the remaining spoonful of vinegar and boiling water. Gradually add the rest of the oil to make a thick, creamy, smooth mayonnaise. If it should curdle, tip the mixture out, clean the goblet and blend another egg yolk in it. Gradually add the first mixture to it. Divide the mixture into two. Add yogurt to half, add herbs to the rest. Put into small dishes and serve with Crudités.

CRUDITÉS

½ cucumber
3 carrots
4 sticks of celery
1 small red or green pepper, deseeded
½ cauliflower
bunch of radishes
breadsticks

Wash and trim vegetables and cut into bite-size pieces. Break breadsticks into 5-cm/2-inch lengths. Arrange on platters around the mayonnaise dips.

ADVENTURE PARTY

An exciting, action-packed party for eight-to-twelve year olds. The theme for this is adventure and the outdoor life. The invitation could be a map, showing the way to "Base Camp" and indicating hazards to be passed on the way, bridges to be crossed, deserts or forests to be traversed and mountains to be scaled!

Improvise an indoor or outdoor "camp" or "den" somewhere for the guests to huddle in when it's time to eat. This could be a bottom bunk bed enclosed by old blankets (remove the bedding first), under a table, in a tent improvised from a blanket over the washing line, sides weighted with bricks. Any smallish, cramped space can be used to good advantage, remember Scott of the Antarctic! Maybe presents could be opened in here too.

It adds to the effect if you can divide the party food into individual ration packs, with each item foil-wrapped and labelled. This could be done during the morning and saves laying the table!

TOILET ROLL WRAPPING

This is a game demanding breathtaking dexterity and patience! Divide the children into teams of six at the most. Each team stands in single file. The person in front holds onto the loose end of a toilet roll but passes the rest over his head to the person behind. He passes it back, and so on, until it reaches the back of the line. The last person has the tricky task of taking the roll down through his or her legs and passing it back to the front between everyone's legs. The team must unwind the whole roll without breaking it, then move forward to get over a line about 10-metres/10-yards in front of them. The first team to get over this line, still linked together with intact toilet roll is the winner!

HANKY HURLING

This is a very strenuous game and can only be played by people with big muscles! Each child attempts to hurl a clean hanky as far as possible from a given line. This is bound to cause great hilarity.

CUT THE ICEBERG

Fill a pudding basin with flour then turn it out onto a large plate or tray. Carefully place a coin on the top. One player at a time, takes a knife and cuts off a slice of the iceberg. The aim is not to dislodge the coin in doing so, but to leave it in such a precarious position that the next person is bound to dislodge it. The first person to dislodge the coin has to pick it up, out of the pile of flour, with his or her mouth. Ugh!

POTHOLE GAME

This sounds like an outside game but need not be. You could create a tunnel with a blanket attached to furniture on either side. Children crawl through the tunnel, under the dining-room chairs arranged in a line along the hall. They must go upstairs backwards, somersault along the landing and put a cross on the chart at the end. The children then hop back along the landing, come down the stairs on their tummies, crawl back through the chairs and along the blanket tunnel. Each person should be timed, and penalty seconds are added if they cheat. Play in teams, totalling up the times, or individually to find one winner.

EAT THE CHOCOLATE

Have ready a hat, scarf, a large pair of gloves, a rather large jacket, and dice. You also need a thick bar of chocolate on an old plate and a knife and fork. The children sit in a circle taking it in turns to throw the dice. Any child that throws a six leaps up, puts on the hat, scarf, jacket and gloves, picks up the knife and fork and attempts to cut and eat as much chocolate as they can. The dice continues to be passed round and as soon as another six is thrown the winner puts on the awkward clothes and has a go. Sometimes, a child won't even have a chance to get the gloves on before another six is thrown, so it becomes a mad rush to get a bite of the chocolate!

POPCORN
Serves 12

If you prefer your popcorn savoury just pour on melted butter, and sprinkle with salt to taste.

About 1 tablespoon oil
6 tablespoons popping corn
75 g/3 oz butter
100 g/4 oz caster sugar

Use a large heavy-based pan with a tight-fitting lid. Add enough oil to just cover the base. Heat the oil and add a tablespoon of popping corn. Cover the pan and shake it gently over a high heat until you hear the corn popping. When popping subsides, tip corn into a bowl. Repeat until you have almost filled a large mixing bowl. Melt the butter in a pan, add the sugar and cook very gently until the sugar dissolves. Continue cooking until golden. Pour over the popcorn and toss lightly. Transport in plastic bags.

MIGHTY MOUNTAIN

1 19-cm/7-inch sponge flan case
1 1 litre round tub of ice cream
4 egg whites
100 g/4 oz caster sugar

Put the flan case onto a flat, ovenproof dish. Dip the tub of ice cream briefly into hot water then turn it out into the flan case. Put this into the freezer. Heat the oven to hot (230°C, 450°F, gas 8). Whisk the egg whites until stiff but not dry and whisk in the sugar a little at a time. Quickly spread the meringue over the ice cream and pull it into peaks. Bake for 5 minutes until the peaks are pale golden brown. Serve immediately.

PIONEER'S PASTIES
Makes 12

Vary the filling according to preferences. Try chicken or fish in a tasty white sauce or even spicy lentils.

225 g/8 oz rindless streaky bacon rashers
1 medium onion, chopped
225 g/8 oz minced beef
227-g/8-oz can baked beans
1 teaspoon Worcestershire sauce
450 g/1 lb shortcrust pastry (i.e. made from
**   450 g/1 lb flour, 225 g/8 oz fat, etc.)**
1 egg, beaten
2 tablespoons milk

Chop the bacon and heat in a saucepan, until the fat runs out. Add onion and cook until pale golden. Stir in beef, cook for 10 minutes, stirring occasionally. Add baked beans and Worcestershire sauce. Mix well and leave to cool. Roll out half the pastry and cut out six 16-cm/5-inch circles. Roll out rest of pastry and cut out another six circles. Divide filling between centres of circles. Brush around the edges with beaten egg. Draw the edges up over the filling and pinch together well to seal. Place on a baking tray and brush with remaining beaten egg mixed with the milk. Cook in a moderately hot oven (200°C, 400°F, gas 6) for 25–30 minutes until crisp and golden. Serve warm or cold.

SCRAMBLES
Makes 12

Pack a few raw carrot sticks or 'Night-Sight Improvers' to eat with these.

6 tablespoons milk
25 g/1 oz butter
10 eggs, beaten
100 g/4 oz sliced ham or salami
½ cucumber, sliced
6 pitta breads

Heat the milk and butter in a non-stick frying pan. Add the eggs and stir over a low heat until very lightly scrambled. Remove from the heat. (The eggs will cook a little more in the heat of the pan). Leave to cool. Cut the ham or salami into strips. Cut the cucumber into matchsticks. Stir lightly into the scrambled egg and season to taste. Cut the pitta breads in half crossways. Open up the two layers of bread to make a pocket. Spoon the mixture inside the pitta pocket. Carefully wrap in cling film to keep pockets closed when being carried.

TEA BREAD
12 slices

This moist, firm fruit loaf is just as good plain as buttered. If possible, store wrapped in foil for a week or so, to mature.

450 ml/¾ pint strong hot tea
200 g/7 oz soft brown sugar
350 g/12 oz mixed dried fruit
275 g/10 oz self-raising flour
1 teaspoon ground mixed spice
1 egg

Mix the tea, sugar and dried fruit in a bowl, cover and leave to soak overnight. Grease a 900 g/2 lb loaf tin and line the bottom with greaseproof paper. Add the flour, spice and egg to the fruit mixture and mix well. Turn into the loaf tin and cook in a moderate oven (180°C, 350°F, gas 4) for about 1 hour 45 minutes. Turn out and cool completely on a wire rack. Slice and serve plain or spread with butter.

MOUNTAINEERS' MINT BISCUITS
Makes 12

Everyone knows that mint is essential on a serious expedition!

50 g/2 oz butter
50 g/2 oz caster sugar
100 g/4 oz flour
175 g/6 oz icing sugar
1–2 tablespoons water
½ teaspoon peppermint flavouring
175 g/6 oz plain dessert chocolate

Beat the butter and caster sugar together until fluffy. Mix in the flour and knead to a smooth dough. Press into a greased 18 × 28-cm/7 × 11-inch Swiss roll tin and prick all over with a fork. Cook in a moderate oven (180°C, 350°F, gas 4) for 10–15 minutes until golden-brown. Allow to cool. Sift the icing sugar into a bowl and mix with enough water to give a spreading consistency. Add the peppermint flavouring, spread over the biscuit base, leave to set. Melt the chocolate in a bowl over a pan of gently simmering water. Spread carefully over the icing and leave to cool. When cold cut into 12 bars.

PEANUT POWER BISCUITS
Makes 50

This is another recipe to make in advance and freeze or store in a tin. Crisp them in a 180°C/350°F/Gas 4 oven for 5 minutes on the party day.

150 g/5 oz butter or margarine
250 g/9 oz plain flour
100 g/4 oz cheese, grated
2 tablespoons water
beaten egg, to glaze
50 g/2 oz chopped salted peanuts

Rub the fat into the flour until the mixture resembles fine breadcrumbs. Stir in the cheese. Add the water, and knead with your fingers to make a firm dough. Knead lightly and roll out to a 25-cm/10-inch square. Trim off edges, cut into 5 strips and place on baking trays leaving space around them. Brush with beaten egg and sprinkle with chopped peanuts, pressing them in lightly. Cut each strip into 5-cm/2-inch squares then cut in half to make triangles. Separate slightly. Cook in a moderate oven (180°C, 350°F, gas 4) for about 20 minutes until pale golden. Transfer carefully to a wire rack to cool.

PANTOMIME PARTY

We suggest an age range of eight to twelve for this party because children of this age have probably been to a pantomime, or may be familiar with the stories.

Give an invitation with some extra fun to it. Write on squares of blotting paper and enclose a bean to grow. Include instructions to curl the blotting paper in a jam jar with the bean sandwiched between paper and glass. Keep the paper moist and the jar in a warm place and the bean will sprout. If you give these out about four weeks before the party, invite guests to bring their living invitation with them and award a prize for the one that's grown the most.

If you can afford a magician to perform for a while, this would add to the atmosphere, otherwise learn a few simple tricks yourself, then you can do a bit of that "oh no he isn't, oh yes he is" routine that children love so much.

This could be a fancy dress party as there are many well-known characters, or put together a dressing-up-box and then they can guess who everybody is supposed to be. Children of this age love to dress up and play active, messy games. We have taken this into account and so should you before embarking on this type of party!

Decorate the house too in a festive way, lots of balloons, masks, fairy lights or disco lights, if you have them.

PIN THE TAIL ON THE PANTO HORSE

Instead of drawing a donkey, draw a crazy panto horse on a large sheet of paper and pin it on the wall. Make a separate tail, perhaps from coloured wools. One child at a time is blindfolded, and given the tail and a piece of Blu-tack so he can try to fix the tail where it belongs. Spin the child round once or twice first, point him or her in the right direction and let them attach the tail. Remove the blindfold so they can see the result!

FIND YOUR PARTNER

This game needs a bit of pre-planning. Either think of pairs of people or one name cut in half. Write the name, or half-name, on a piece of paper and supply safety pins. Pin one name on each child's back without him or her seeing it, and set them off to find their partner. They can only ask the others questions that require yes or no answers and can't ask them all of the same person. As the game progresses, they should find out who they are so they can find their partner or other half!

FACE PAINTING

You can buy face paints in most toy shops or large stationers. Children love playing with them. Get them to make themselves, or a partner, look like someone from a pantomime or nursery rhyme. The session could be at the start of the party or at the end as the reserve game.

PUSS-IN-BOOTS

One of the children is Puss-in-Boots—put him or her in the middle of the ring of children. All are sitting down, except for the cat. The cat has to crawl around getting the children to stroke him or her by meowing at them. They must stroke the cat while it makes funny faces at them, but they must *not* laugh. The cat is not allowed to stay too long in front of one person, and anyone who laughs, in turn becomes the cat.

PUSS-IN-BOOTS PATE

Serves 12

This simple pâté keeps well in the fridge for several days but it is best served at room temperature.

2 120-g/4½-oz cans sardines in oil
225 g/8 oz curd cheese
1 tablespoon lemon juice
2 tablespoons tomato ketchup

Drain the oil from the cans. Split open the sardines and remove the backbones. Put the flesh into a bowl and add the curd cheese, lemon juice and ketchup. Mash the ingredients together with a fork to give a fairly smooth, even texture. Season to taste and spoon into a serving bowl. Serve with Melba Toast.

MELBA TOAST

12 slices of bread

Toast the bread on both sides. Cut off the crusts, then, working quickly, slide a knife into the side of each slice to cut the bread in half through its thickness. Cut each thin slice into triangles then toast each on the unbrowned side. Watch the toast carefully as it tends to curl up and burn quickly. Serve hot or cold to dip into Puss-in-Boots Pâté.

JACK AND THE BEANSTALK

1 shallow 25-cm/10-inch round cake, use size
   three cake mix (see page 6)
1 quantity chocolate butter icing
1 quantity decoration icing
assorted food colourings

Bake the cake for 35–40 minutes. Turn the cake out onto a board or plate. Spread the butter icing over the cake to cover it completely. Colour a quarter of the decoration icing pink and model Jack's hands and head. Add decoration icing 'hair'. Colour the rest of the icing green. Reserve a little for the stalks. Roll out the rest thinly and cut out the leaves. Curl some over a rolling pin and leave to set.

Put Jack's hands and head in the centre of the cake, so he looks as if he is just climbing out of the beanstalk. Paint his features and hair. Arrange the leaves around him and paint in the leaf details with green colouring. Roll reserved green icing into sausages and place them between leaves to represent stalks.

HOT SANDWICH CURLS
Serves 12

If possible serve these warm. They could be keeping warm in the oven during the first half of the party ready for tea.

12 slices bread, thinly sliced
50 g/2 oz butter
cheese spread
peanut butter
yeast or beef extract
jam

Cut the crusts off the bread and spread with butter. Choose one or more fillings from those above or another one your child particularly likes and spread over the bread. Roll up the slice tightly like a Swiss roll, wrap in cling film and chill for about 1 hour. Cut the rolls into 2.5-cm/1-inch thick slices. Pack them tightly, join downwards, on baking trays. Bake in a hot oven (220°C, 425°F, gas 7) for about 10 minutes until crisp and golden.

CORNED BEEF BUTTONS
Makes 36

Children seem to love to nibble on a thick wedge of cucumber. These stuffed slices add a refreshing contrast to the rest of the spread.

2 long, fat cucumbers
198-g/7-oz can corned beef
4 tablespoons tomato ketchup
few drops of Worcestershire sauce

Cut the ends off the cucumbers. Cut each one into 18 thick slices. Put the corned beef into a bowl and remove any excess fat from the edges. Mash beef with a fork, working in the ketchup, Worcestershire sauce and seasoning to taste. Using a small pastry cutter or teaspoon, remove seeds from the centre of the cucumber slices. Spread the corned beef into the centres, piling it up tightly. Chill until required.

GOLDEN EGGS
Serves 12

12 hard-boiled eggs
6 tablespoons mayonnaise
½ teaspoon mild curry powder
paprika

Cut the eggs in half lengthways, remove the yolks and put in a bowl. Add the mayonnaise, curry powder and seasoning and mash together with a fork until smooth. Pipe or carefully spoon the mixture back into the egg whites. Top each with a tiny pinch of paprika.

ROSY APPLES
Makes 12

Allow one apple per child, try to choose nice rosy ones!

900 g/2 lb demerara sugar
100 g/4 oz butter
3 teaspoons vinegar
2 tablespoons golden syrup
300 ml/½ pint water
12 medium-size rosy apples
12 wooden sticks

Put the sugar, butter, vinegar, syrup and water into a large, heavy-based saucepan. Heat gently, stirring occasionally until the sugar has completely dissolved. Stop stirring and bring to the boil. Boil rapidly for 10 minutes or until the temperature reaches 143°C/290°F (soft-crack stage) on a sugar-boiling thermometer. To test without a thermometer, remove pan from heat. Drop a little syrup into iced water. If you can stretch it between your fingers into elastic, but firm strands, it is ready. Remove from heat. Wipe the apples and push the wooden sticks into the cores. Dip the apples into the toffee, twirl around so they are evenly coated. Leave to cool on a buttered baking tray or waxed paper.

UGLY SISTER BISCUITS
Makes 24

If the children at the party are old enough, let them do the decorating, and perhaps give a prize for the ugliest!

175 g/6 oz plain flour
100 g/4 oz butter or margarine
50 g/2 oz caster sugar

To decorate
100 g/4 oz butter
225 g/8 oz icing sugar
1 teaspoon cocoa powder
pink edible food colouring
a selection of small sweets
chocolate vermicelli

Sift flour into a bowl, add the caster sugar and the fat. Rub in until the mixture resembles fine bread-crumbs. Knead mixture together to form a fairly firm dough. Turn out onto a lightly-floured board and knead lightly until smooth. Roll out and stamp out circles with a 5-cm/2-inch pastry cutter. Arrange on a greased baking tray. Cook in a moderately hot oven (190°C, 375°F, gas 5) for 15 minutes until pale golden and firm. Allow to cool for five minutes before transferring to a wire rack. To decorate, beat butter and icing sugar together, until smooth. Colour a quarter of the icing brown with the cocoa. Colour another quarter pink. Put the icings into grease-proof paper piping bags and snip off the tips. Pipe hair and features onto the biscuits (remembering to make them ugly!) and finish with sweets and chocolate vermicelli.

'EAT ME'

INTERNATIONAL SPY PARTY

This is a party for older children, aged about ten to twelve. It offers wonderful scope as a fancy dress party and both girls and boys will love disguising themselves and dressing up to suit the theme. The games suggested require a bit of forethought and preparation but this is mainly because older children like more of a challenge. Besides, they are almost too old to have organised parties so make the last one really memorable!

The invitations can be written in invisible ink or written in code (providing the decoding information is available). The recipients will enjoy deciphering the message and think what fun they can have composing a reply!

All presents should be smuggled in, and the birthday child will have to 'frisk' the guests to find it. Parents could dress up as well (providing their child won't be embarassed about it) to add to the fun and spirit of the party.

The house could be decorated appropriately with maps, secret plans, darkened rooms and sultry music.

The food has an international theme. Our American and Russian-influenced spread could be supplemented with poppadoms, prawn crackers and Bombay mix to nibble.

The games we've suggested are quite hectic so remember this when deciding how many to invite.

CHOPSTICKS AND PEANUTS

Chopsticks have been used in this game to carry on the international theme. Using chopsticks, the children must transfer as many peanuts as possible from one bowl to another. This game can either be played in teams, setting a time limit for each person, or individually, seeing who can transfer the most in one minute. You can play a variation with a straw, where children attempt to move the peanuts by suction.

CHINESE WHISPERS

The children stand in line and the first person whispers a message in the next person's ear. The message is then repeated on down the line. The last person to receive the message speaks it out loud. You will rarely find it's the same sentence that started out! Repeat until everyone has had the chance to pass on their own message.

POSTING GAME

Before the party, find eight jam jars and label them clearly with the name of a city anywhere in the world. Dot the jam jars around the house or garden but don't make them too hard to find. Cut up a lot of other scraps of paper and write the name of each city on about 24 pieces. (ie. 24 slips with Istanbul, 24 with New York etc.). Mix them up. When the game begins, give one slip to every child at random. They must put their name on it (remember to have a supply of pencils ready) then rush to find the right jar and post their 'slip' into it. They can then rush back for another one and the winner is the one who posts the most in the right pots. This game is very hectic and older children love it. Set a time limit so when you shout "five minutes" they panic, "two minutes" and they are all out of breath! The count down makes it all the more exciting.

PASSPORT CONSEQUENCES

Children of this age have often played normal consequences and this is a slight adaptation. Each child needs a strip of paper and they start by writing a name at the top. They then have to fold over this piece and pass the paper on to the next person who has to write their nationality (real or imagined), fold over and pass on. Add a brief description and pass on. The next people add who they are meeting, nationality, description, then where, finally what the outcome was. This continues the spy theme and should be done as secretly as possible. Read aloud at the end.

FRONTIER GAME

Each 'spy' has the name of a different famous person pinned to his or her back but they don't know who they are. They must circulate asking each other questions that give clues to their own identity i.e. Am I male or female/young or old, etc. They can only ask one question of one person at a time and must continue until they have all guessed who they are.

RAILWAY CARRIAGE GAME

You'll need to prepare this game before the party starts. Save newspapers for several days. (If you can get hold of some foreign papers so much the better). Rearrange the pages of each of the papers so that they are no longer in numerical order, some are upside-down, some back-to-front. Seat six children, three abreast facing each other in a hallway. (It's more fun in a confined space). They are now in the railway carriage and need to put the paper back in its proper order whilst sitting cramped together. This is the most hilarious game, absolute chaos, with pages everywhere and everybody shouting at each other. Obviously the first one to finish wins, but anyone who manages it deserves a prize!

TOP SECRET

1 28 × 18 × 4-cm/11 × 7 × 1½-inch cake, use
** size two cake mix (see page 6)**
4 tablespoons apricot jam, warmed
2 quantities decoration icing
assorted food colourings

Bake the cake for 25–35 minutes. Turn out the cake onto a board. Cut a 2.5-cm/1-inch strip off the shorter edge and put aside. Spread the jam over the cake. Roll out one quantity of icing and cover the whole cake. Colour a quarter of the decoration icing blue, another quarter buff. Roll it out thinly and cut into large squares. Arrange them on the cake, like papers on a desk, rolling up one to resemble a plan. Cut 10-cm/4-inch piece from the reserved strip of cake. Wrap it in decoration icing to make the camera body. Cover a small round piece for the lens. Stick the two pieces together with a little egg white. Place them on the cake. Paint the 'desk' with brown food colouring. Paint details on plans and papers with a fine paintbrush. Paint the camera black or brown, paint camera details and decoration icing keys with silver food colouring. Leave to dry.

CHICAGO PIZZA
Serves 12

Older children have notoriously large appetites. You may need to make two of these!

283-g/10-oz packet bread mix
3 tablespoons oil
1 large onion, thinly sliced
100 g/4 oz button mushrooms, sliced
4 tablespoons tomato purée
100 g/4 oz sliced ham
225 g/8 oz grated cheese
4 tablespoons milk

Make up the bread mix according to the directions on the packet. Roll out dough to a 30-cm/12-inch round. Slide onto an oiled baking tray, cover with oiled cling film and leave to rise in a warm place for 30 minutes. Meanwhile, heat the oil in a frying pan and fry the onions until transparent. Add the mushrooms and cook for a further 5 minutes. Stir in the tomato purée and season to taste. Spread the tomato mixture over the pizza. Cut the ham into strips and scatter over. Combine the grated cheese and milk and spread over the pizza. Cook in a moderately hot oven (200°C, 400°F, gas 6) for 20 minutes, then reduce the heat to 180°C, 350°F, gas 4 and cook for a further 15–20 minutes. Serve hot with Coleslaw.

COLESLAW

325 g/12 oz red and/or white cabbage
4 carrots
2 sticks celery
150 ml/¼ pint mayonnaise or salad cream

Trim the cabbage and shred very finely. Grate the carrots, thinly slice the celery. Toss all the vegetables together with mayonnaise or salad cream until evenly coated. Allow to soften for an hour or so before serving.

AMERICAN BROWNIES
Makes 12

225 g/8 oz butter or margarine
1 teaspoon vanilla essence
350 g/13 oz caster sugar
4 eggs
100 g/4 oz plain flour
75 g/3 oz cocoa powder
½ teaspoon baking powder
100 g/4oz walnuts, roughly chopped

Put the butter and vanilla essence in a large bowl and place over a pan of gently simmering water. Stir until melted. Remove from the pan and allow to cool. Add the sugar. Add the eggs, one at a time, beating well after each addition. Carefully fold in the flour, cocoa and baking powder, then the walnuts. Pour the mixture into a greased and base-lined 28 × 18 × 4-cm/11 × 7 × 1½-inch tin and smooth the top. Cook in a moderate oven (180°C, 350°F, gas 4) for 50 minutes or until firm. Leave to cool in the tin, then cut into 12 pieces.

PILAFSKI
Serves 12

4 tablespoons oil
350 g/12 oz cracked wheat or burghul
1 onion, finely chopped
900 ml/1½ pints strong chicken stock
2 tablespoons chopped parsley

Heat the oil in a saucepan and add the cracked wheat or bulgur and onion. Cook, stirring occasionally, until the cracked wheat or bulgur begins to brown. Add the stock and seasoning and bring to the boil. Cover and cook on a low heat for about 10 minutes, until all the stock has been absorbed. Remove from the heat and allow to stand, covered, for a further 10 minutes to give a fluffier texture. Spread on a large platter, sprinkle with parsley, and top with Meatballskis.

MEATBALLSKIS
Serves 12

450 g/1 lb minced beef
1 onion, finely chopped
3 tablespoons chopped parsley
50 g/2 oz fresh breadcrumbs
1 egg

Put the minced beef, onion, parsley, breadcrumbs, egg and plenty of seasoning into a bowl. Mix thoroughly with a wooden spoon (or your hands). Shape into walnut-sized balls between wet hands and place on a baking tray. Cook in a moderately hot oven (190°C, 375°F, gas 5) for about 30 minutes until brown and crisp. Serve with cracked wheat Pilafski.

ORANGE GRENADES
Makes 12

12 medium, unblemished oranges
175 g/6 oz caster sugar
600 ml/1 pint double cream
12 cocktail cherries
12 cocktail sticks

Cut a very thin slice from the base of each orange so they will stand up. Cut a lid from the top of each and reserve. Scrape out all the flesh from the oranges and reserve the shells. Put the fruit in a nylon sieve and press out the juice with the back of a wooden spoon. Measure out 450 ml/¾ pint juice, add the sugar and stir until dissolved. Whip the cream until it just forms soft peaks. Gradually whisk in the orange juice. Pour into a shallow container and freeze for 3–4 hours until beginning to freeze around the edges. Beat the ice cream until smooth again, then quickly spoon it into the orange shells. Replace the lids and freeze the oranges until required (up to 2 months).

Transfer to the fridge 15 minutes before serving, to soften slightly. Spear a cherry on a cocktail stick and push diagonally through the lid into the orange for the 'pin'!

TOPSY-TURVY PARTY

This is a party for children aged between six and ten, and it should be one long laugh from beginning to end, especially if the organiser is in a jolly mood! Start with the invitations, written in some confused way, with some letters upside-down, names back to front, or even writing in a spiral. Use paper that has another, obvious use like loo roll, kitchen towel or the edge of a newspaper. Leave a space at the end for the reply but start a crazy sentence for the guest to finish. For example, 'Hateful Holly, I have got my wellingtons on but . . . .' should get some interesting responses!

It is the ideal opportunity for the parents to dress up, topsy-turvy style. Wear trousers inside-out, shirt back to front with the tie at the back, odd shoes, socks worn like mittens, etc, etc. This could turn into a wonderful game, as two teams race to re-arrange their topsy-turvy people. If you can't face it, you could use dolls, or ask for volunteers among the children. As guests arrive, have them throw any cards and presents into a waste-paper basket (not advisable with small children though, as they take present-giving very seriously!).

Make the food topsy-turvy to fit the theme. The trifle is upside-down, the cherries on the bottoms of the cakes and the filling on the outside of the sandwiches. The cake, a clown peeping back through his legs, is upside-down too. See if you can sing Happy Birthday backwards before the birthday person blows out the candles!

The games we've suggested can be played indoors, but it is always a good idea to use the garden if possible. Lots are familiar games, but played with a slight variation. They do require a bit of thinking about in advance, but then all party games need some sort of props.

BLIND EVERYBODY'S BUFF

You know how to play Blind Man's Buff, well in this game *everyone* is blindfolded. The children feel their way around trying to catch each other. When they find someone, they take off their blindfolds and try and avoid being caught.

MUSICAL STAND-UPS

Musical bumps—but in reverse! The children start off sitting down, and when the music stops they have to stand up. Last one on their feet is out. Start the music again when they're all sitting. Absolutely exhausting!

LEFT-HAND DRAWING

Paper and pencils are required for this game. The grown-up in charge whispers to one of the children something to draw. The child has to draw it using the hand he or she doesn't normally write with. Whoever guesses what it is being illustrated first becomes the artist. Suitable for any age, just make the subjects as hard or as easy as you think appropriate.

BACKWARD WHEELBARROW RACE

You need to be outside or have a large hall for this game! It is just like any wheelbarrow race—except they must go backwards.

TOPSY TURNOVERS
Makes 12

25 g/1 oz butter
3 tablespoons plain flour
150 ml/¼ pint milk
½ chicken stock cube
2 rindless rashers streaky bacon, chopped
175 g/6 oz boneless cooked chicken
370-g/13-oz frozen puff pastry, thawed
1 egg, beaten

Heat the butter in a saucepan. Fry the bacon until crisp. Add the flour and cook for 1 minute. Gradually add the milk and bring to the boil, stirring. Add the stock cube and cook for 1 minute. Remove from the heat. Finely chop the chicken, add to the sauce and season to taste. Roll out the pastry and cut out twelve 10-cm/4-inch squares. Divide the chicken mixture between them. Brush the edges with beaten egg and fold the turnovers in half diagonally. Arrange on a dampened baking tray and glaze with egg. Cook in a preheated moderately hot oven (200°C, 400°F, gas 6) for about 30 minutes until crisp and golden. Serve hot or cold.

TOPSY THE CLOWN

1 25-cm/10-inch square cake, use size three cake mix (see page 6)
1 quantity butter icing
red and pink food colouring
½ quantity decoration icing
thin liquorice strips
assorted sweets

Bake the cake for 35–40 minutes. Put the cake onto a board. Arrange it so that one corner is in the centre of the top edge; this becomes the clown's hat. Round off the two corners at the sides of the board to shape the trousers and trim the bottom edge level. The pieces cut from the sides tuck into the base to become his shoes. Use a little butter icing to stick the pieces together. Cover the whole cake with most of the butter icing. Colour two tablespoons of butter icing pink. Spread it over his face. Place liquorice strips around edges and make frills, shoe laces and features. Decorate his trousers with small sweets. Colour the remaining butter icing red and pipe on his hair, mouth and hat pompoms. Colour the decoration icing pink and shape into eight pink fingers. Wrap them around his ankles.

SAUSAGE ROLL-UPS
Makes 12

12 thin slices brown bread
butter
6 tablespoons sweet pickle
12 pork chipolatas
24 wooden cocktail sticks

Cut the crusts off the bread and roll the bread slices flatter with a rolling pin. Butter the bread thinly and spread with the pickle. Put a sausage on each piece of bread and roll up tightly. Secure each with two cocktail sticks. Place on a greased baking tray and cook in a moderate oven (180°C, 350°F, gas 4) for 25–30 minutes until crisp and golden. Serve warm.

INSIDE-OUT SANDWICHES
Makes 36

These festive looking 'sandwiches' have their filling on the outside.

2 thin sesame seed loaves
butter
100 g/4 oz liver pâté
100 g/4 oz cottage cheese
225-g/8-oz can pilchards in tomato sauce

To garnish
tomato, cucumber, midget gherkins, hard-boiled egg slices, radishes, crispy-grilled bacon, salad cress

Cut thirty-six thin slices of bread and spread with butter. Spread twelve slices with liver pâté and twelve with cottage cheese. Drain and mash pilchards and spread on remaining slices. Cut thin slices of tomato, cucumber and radish and arrange on some of the sandwiches. Cut gherkins into fans and use to garnish the liver pâté, crumble the bacon over the cottage cheese. Chop white of the hard-boiled egg, sieve the yolk. Sprinkle over the pilchards. Arrange the sandwiches on a serving plate and sprinkle with a little salad cress.

UPSIDE-DOWN CAKES
Makes 24

175 g/6 oz butter or margarine
175 g/6 oz caster sugar
3 eggs
175 g/6 oz self-raising flour
grated rind of ½ orange
paper cake cases

To decorate
100 g/4 oz icing sugar
1 tablespoon orange juice
12 glacé cherries

Beat the fat, sugar, eggs and flour together for 2–3 minutes until light and fluffy. Beat in the orange rind. Stand the paper cake cases in bun tins and divide the mixture between them. Bake in a moderately hot oven (190°C, 375°F, gas 5) for about 20 minutes until firm to the touch. Cool in cases, on a wire rack. Beat icing sugar and orange juice together to make a stiff glacé icing. Remove paper cases from cakes. Spoon icing over the *bottom* of each cake and top with half a glacé cherry.

ICED-UNDER BISCUITS
Makes 24

175 g /6 oz digestive biscuits
100 g/4 oz caster sugar
100 g/4 oz margarine
50 g/2 oz cocoa powder
1 egg, beaten
100 g /4 oz chocolate-flavoured cake covering

Put the biscuits in a plastic bag and roughly crush them with a rolling pin. Gently heat the sugar, margarine and cocoa in a saucepan. When the margarine has melted, remove the pan from the heat and mix in the egg and crushed biscuits. Press the mixture firmly into a greased 18 × 28-cm/7 × 11-inch Swiss roll tin. Smooth the top. Break the chocolate cake covering into pieces and melt it in a bowl over a pan of hot water. Spread over the biscuit mixture and mark with a fork. Leave to set. Cut into thin fingers. Arrange chocolate-side down on a plate.

TOPSY-TURVY TRIFLE
Serves 12

4 tablespoons custard powder
2 tablespoons sugar
900 ml/1½ pints milk
2 packets tangerine jelly
2 312-g/11-oz cans mandarin oranges
3 bananas
6 mini jam-filled Swiss rolls

Blend custard powder and sugar with a little of the milk. Heat the remaining milk until almost boiling, and pour onto the custard powder, stirring constantly. Return the custard to the rinsed-out pan and bring to the boil stirring. Cook for 2 minutes. Allow to cool slightly, then pour the custard into a 2 litre/4 pint glass dish. Break up the jelly tablets, put them in a pan with 150 ml/¼ pint water and heat until melted. Drain syrup from mandarins. Make up to 600 ml/1 pint with water. Add to the jelly. Slice the Swiss rolls. Arrange slices neatly on the custard with the oranges and sliced bananas. Spoon some jelly over the Swiss roll to soak it so it won't float to the surface. Pour the jelly over and chill until set.

PICNIC PARTY

This party idea is suitable for any age group, but dry weather is essential. If you are taking younger children then you will certainly need help, not just for laying out the picnic and organising games, but, especially where very young children are concerned, keeping an eye on their whereabouts. If there is a wood nearby there will be trees to climb as well as organised games. An adventure playground is fun for all ages if you are lucky enough to have one near.

Make an invitation to look like a picnic hamper from a piece of paper folded like an envelope. Inside, put drawings or cut-outs of food and space for a reply. Or, make the invitation look like a ticket, either one to ride or an admission ticket. Bear in mind that transport may be necessary. If going by bus, don't make it too long a journey, and have some entertainment in mind such as 'I Spy'. If you're travelling by car, a sing-song keeps them going, but again, don't travel too far or the children get bored.

Obviously, the food will have to be transported too. We have taken this into account in the recipes. You may need to borrow coolboxes and picnicware to cater for party numbers.

WHAT'S THE TIME Mr. WOLF?

Most children know this game. One stands out in front with his back to the others who gradually creep up on him chanting "What's the time Mr. Wolf?" He turns to face them saying "It's - - - o'clock". Then he turns back, the children start creeping up again, still asking the time. When he calls out "Dinner Time!", he rushes to catch them before they can run back to their base. Whoever he catches takes his place and the game starts again.

KNOTS

One child is made to turn his back for a few minutes while the others group into fours or sixes and join hands in circles. The members of the circles tie themselves together by stepping over and under arms, and twisting around, but they must not let go of each other. The "un-knotter" then turns round and has to untie them without breaking the circle.

LADDERS

Sit the children on the ground in teams facing each other, legs outstretched and feet touching those of an opposing team member so their legs make a ladder. The organiser numbers each couple, then shouts numbers at random. The numbered pair leaps up, race up the 'ladder', around their own side of it, and

back up to their original place. Meanwhile, another number has been called but a child cannot run until the last runner in his or her own team has sat down, like a relay race. The winners are the team that are all sitting first.

PICNIC BUNS
Makes 12

283-g/10-oz packet white bread mix
6 tablespoons milk
6 tablespoons demerara sugar
225 g/8 oz currants
4 teaspoons mixed spice
1 teaspoon poppy seeds
225 g/8 oz icing sugar, sifted
2-4 teaspoons lemon juice
12 glacé cherries, cut into quarters

Make the bread mix into a dough according to the directions on the packet. Roll it out to a 45 × 30-cm/18 × 12-inch rectangle. Brush half the milk over the dough. Sprinkle the dough with the sugar, currants and spices. Roll up the dough as tightly as you can. Cut it into 12 4-cm/1½-inch slices. Place them cut side up on a greased baking tray and flatten them slightly until they are almost touching but leave room for them to rise. Cover them with oiled cling film and leave them in a warm place until doubled in size. Brush them with the remaining milk. Bake in a hot oven (230°C, 450°F, gas 8) for 15–20 minutes until golden brown. Cool. Mix the icing sugar with enough lemon juice to give a coating consistency. Drizzle the icing over the buns and decorate with quartered glacé cherries.

MUESLI FLAPJACKS
Makes 12

100 g/4 oz butter or margarine
4 tablespoons clear honey
50 g/2 oz soft brown sugar
225 g/8 oz muesli
50 g/2 oz dried apricots, chopped

Melt the fat, honey and sugar in a saucepan. Stir in the muesli and chopped apricots. Spread the mixture into a greased 18 × 28-cm/7 × 11-inch Swiss roll tin. Smooth the top and bake in a moderate oven (180°C, 350°F, gas 4) for 20–25 minutes until golden. Allow to cool in the tin for 10 minutes before cutting into 12 bars and transferring to a wire rack.

Dear Heather
Would you like to come to my picnic
party on Saturday 14th May, 3-5pm.
Meet at my h___ ___ we go out.
Sydney ___
___ Ma___

TEA

crisps

THIS IS YOUR TICKET TO
A PICNIC PARTY ON SAT.
14TH MAY. 3-5pm.
MEET AT 15. SYDNEY ST.
PARTY SPECIA___
FROM   RETURN

THIS IS YOUR TICKET TO
MY PICNIC PARTY ON SATURDAY!
14TH MAY. 3-5pm. MEET AT
15, SYDNEY STREET.
PARTY SPECIAL
FROM MARY
12345678

TEAR HERE

MINI-QUICHES
Makes 24

225 g/8 oz shortcrust pastry
8 rashers rindless streaky bacon
175 g/6 oz grated cheese
3 eggs
300 ml/½ pint milk
salt and pepper
6 spring onions, trimmed, and sliced crosswise

Roll out the pastry, stamp out 24 circles with a 7.5-cm/3-inch cutter and line bun tins with the pastry circles. Chop the bacon and fry in a non-stick pan until it begins to sizzle. Add the spring onions. Fry together for 5 minutes, then divide the mixture between the pastry cases. Top each with a little grated cheese. Beat the eggs and milk together. Season and pour into the pastry cases. Bake in a moderate oven (180°C, 350°F, gas 4) for 20–25 minutes until set. Serve cold.

SUN'S-OUT PIE
Serves 12

These cheery picnic rolls reveal their sunny interiors when sliced. Take them along whole, and slice at the picnic site.

2 370-g/13-oz packets frozen puff pastry,
**   thawed**
450 g/1 lb sausagemeat
1 large onion, finely chopped
225 g/8 oz cheese, grated
25 g/1 oz fresh breadcrumbs
2 eggs, beaten
6 eggs, hard-boiled
milk to glaze

Carefully roll out each piece of pastry into a 35.5 × 25.5-cm/14 × 10-inch rectangle. Place the rectangles on dampened baking trays. Mix the sausagemeat, onion, cheese, breadcrumbs and beaten eggs together, adding plenty of seasoning. Spread a quarter of the mixture in a 5 cm/2 inch wide strip along the centre of each pastry oblong. Halve the hard-boiled eggs lengthways. Place end to end, cut side up, on top of the sausagemeat. Carefully cover with the rest of the sausagemeat, packing it neatly into a sausage shape. Damp the edges of the pastry and seal together. Turn rolls over, so the seams are underneath. Brush pastry with milk and cook in a preheated moderately hot oven (200°C, 400°F, gas 6) for 40 minutes. Serve cold, cut into thick slices.

CARROT CAKE
Serves 12

225 g/8 oz self-raising flour
2 teaspoons baking powder
150 g/5 oz soft brown sugar
50 g/2 oz walnuts, chopped
225 g/8 oz carrots, grated
2 small ripe bananas, mashed
2 eggs
150 ml/¼ pint corn oil

Topping
75 g/3 oz cream cheese
75 g/3 oz icing sugar, sifted

Sift the flour and baking powder into a large bowl and stir in the brown sugar and walnuts. Squeeze any excess moisture out of the carrots and add with the bananas. Stir together. Lightly beat the eggs and oil, then gradually beat them into the mixture with a wooden spoon. Grease a deep 18-cm/7-inch square cake tin and line the bottom with greaseproof paper. Spoon cake mixture into tin and smooth the top. Cook in a moderate oven (180°C, 350°F, gas 4) for about 1¼ hours until a skewer inserted into the middle of the cake comes out clean. Turn out and allow to cool on a wire rack. Beat cream cheese and icing sugar together. Split cake in half. Spread mixture over the base then sandwich together again. Cut into 12 pieces.

TAKE-OUT BURGERS
Makes 12

Hamburger buns can be too large for young children, so choose a smaller soft roll for them. If you are making the burgers in advance, wrap them in foil, and write the owners' names on them. If you have plenty of adult helpers and a portable barbecue, you could cook the burgers at the picnic site.

12 beefburgers
12 hamburger buns
about 3 tablespoons mayonnaise
12 lettuce leaves
about 4 tablespoons hamburger relish
2 dill pickles, sliced

Grill the beefburgers for 2–3 minutes each side. Cool. Split the buns open and toast the cut sides. Spread mayonnaise on the base of the bun. Put the lettuce leaf on top, then the burger. Top with a generous spoonful of hamburger relish and a slice of dill pickle.

THE WIZARD OF OZ

The age range of this party is large because of the recent revival of interest in the Wizard of Oz story. Adapt the games, if necessary, for younger children, making one or two of them simpler—fewer items in the memory game, for instance. The story is one of fantasy and magic, so you could create this sort of atmosphere in the house with subdued lighting and quiet music. Hang foil stars and moons on cotton thread from the ceiling. You'll need plenty of large balloons too, as the Wizard leaves in one at the end of the story. The balloon theme starts with the invitations. Write the party details on a thin piece of paper, roll it up tightly, and slip it inside a large balloon. Inflate the balloon and tie it tightly. The recipients will have to burst it to retrieve the invite!

You may choose to make this a fancy dress party, and we recommend you address the children as Munchkins throughout the party. After all, that is what they have come for, a good munch! The food and the games are inspired by the story.

TIN MAN'S HEART

'Pin the tail on the donkey' with a difference. Get your child to lie on a piece of wallpaper. Draw round him or her to get a basic outline for the tin man, then add a funnel-shaped hat. Spray it silver if you have the time or inclination and add face, seams and rivets. Hang him on the wall. Draw a square where his heart should be. Cut out a red heart-shape. Each child, in turn, is blindfolded, and has to stick the heart in the right place (use Blu-tack.) The one closest to the centre of the square wins.

WITCH'S SLIPPER

Sit the children in a circle on the floor. One takes the centre, is blindfolded and becomes the witch. The others pass a shoe continuously around the circle. The witch must listen carefully to discover which person is holding it. When he or she points at the right person, the two swap places.

BRICK ROAD RACE

You will need four bricks, preferably yellow! Divide the children into two teams. Half of each team stands at each end of a marked course about 20-metres/20-yards long. One child from each team is given two bricks, and they have to race each other to the other end of the course by using the bricks as stepping stones and moving them along. They must not step on the floor. At the other end, another team member takes over, and races back. First team home wins!

MEMORY GAME

The scarecrow thinks he has no brain and that is the inspiration for this game. A tray of objects is presented to the children and they have two minutes to memorise the items on it. (The older the children, the more objects on the tray). When you remove the tray from sight they must write down as many things as they can remember.

DOROTHY'S DRAWINGS

Divide the children into two teams. One child from each team comes to you, and you whisper to them the name of a book, a nursery rhyme or an object. They must return to their teams and draw a picture to communicate what you have whispered. The first team to guess the answer wins. Then two more children have a turn.

CYCLONE PUDDINGS

Serves 12

Use disposable transparent plastic beakers for this pud so the 'cyclone' effect is visible.

2 400-g/14.1-oz cans raspberries or loganberries
2 packets raspberry jelly
150 ml/¼ pint whipping cream

Drain fruit, reserving syrup from cans. Make it up to 600 ml/1 pint with water. Break the jelly tablets into cubes and heat them in 150 ml/¼ pint of the syrup until melted. Add the fruit and remaining syrup and chill until beginning to set. Fork the jelly lightly then pour it into transparent plastic beakers. Pour a little cream over each and quickly give a light stir to swirl it through the jelly. Chill until set.

WIZARD'S BALLOON

1 15 × 15 × 7.5-cm/6 × 6 × 3-inch cake, use size two cake mix (see page 6)
1 quantity coffee-flavoured butter icing
1 teaspoon cocoa powder
sweets to fill 'basket'
4 straws
1 large balloon
adhesive stars

Bake the cake for 35–40 minutes. Turn the cake upside-down on a cake board. Reserve 2 tablespoons butter icing; use the rest to cover the whole cake. Smooth it with a palette knife. Use the tines of a fork to mark the sides to resemble basketwork. Work in rows, alternating vertical and horizontal lines. Mix the cocoa into the remaining butter icing and pipe around top and bottom edges and corners. Fill the centre of the 'basket' with sweets. Press the four straws into the cake at a 60° angle so they will support the inflated balloon. Stick stars onto the balloon, then place it in position on the cake.

MAGIC CIRCLES
Makes 24

When is a circle not a circle? When it becomes a tasty triangle! Of course, you can use fresh smoked haddock poached in enough milk to cover, for 5 minutes. Use the poaching milk instead of the fresh milk to make the sauce.

212-g/7½-oz packet boil-in-the-bag smoked haddock
25 g/1 oz butter
3 tablespoons plain flour
150 ml/¼ pint milk
2 hard-boiled eggs
1 tablespoon chopped parsley
370-g/13-oz packet frozen puff pastry, thawed
1 egg, beaten

Cook the haddock according to the directions on the packet. Heat the butter in a saucepan, add the flour and cook, stirring constantly, for 1 minute. Add the milk gradually, stirring constantly. Bring to the boil, stirring. Cook for 2 minutes, remove from the heat. Flake the fish, discarding skin and bones. Shell and chop the hard-boiled eggs. Add with the fish and parsley to the sauce. Season to taste. Roll out the pastry thinly and stamp out circles with a 7.5-cm/3-inch pastry cutter. Spoon a little fish mixture in the centre of each circle. Brush the edge with beaten egg and fold the sides of pastry in over the filling to shape into a triangle. Pinch corners to seal firmly. Arrange on a dampened baking tray and brush with beaten egg. Cook in a preheated moderately hot oven (200°C, 400°F, gas 6) for about 20 minutes until crisp and golden. Serve warm or cold.

HOT TOTOS
Makes 12

Toto, as every Oz fan knows, is Dorothy's dog!

12 frankfurters
12 soft finger rolls
butter
tomato ketchup or mild mustard
3 tomatoes, quartered
12 small gherkins
cocktail sticks

Grill the frankfurters for about 5 minutes, turning them once or twice. Split the rolls lengthways, but do not separate the two halves. Spread thinly with butter

and a little ketchup or mustard and put a frankfurter inside. Spear each hot dog roll with a tomato quarter and gherkin threaded on a cocktail stick.

YELLOW BRICKS
Serves 12

225 g/8 oz self-raising flour
¼ teaspoon salt
½ teaspoon dry mustard
25 g/1 oz butter
100 g/4 oz grated Cheddar cheese
150 ml/¼ pint milk
150-g/5.3-oz tube cheese spread with ham
1 tub of salad cress

Sift the flour, salt and mustard into a mixing bowl and rub in the butter. Add three-quarters of the cheese and bind with the milk to form a soft dough. Roll out lightly into a 20 × 15-cm/8 × 6-inch rectangle, and cut into 12 'bricks'. Place these on a greased baking sheet, brush with milk and sprinkle with the remaining cheese. Cook in a hot oven (220°C, 425°F, gas 7) for about 12 minutes until well-risen and golden. Cool on a wire rack, split and spread bottom half thickly with cheese spread. Garnish with a little cress. Stick the two halves together again.

SUNSHINE BUNS
Makes 12

75 g/3 oz butter
1 egg, beaten
2 tablespoons milk
75 g/3 oz caster sugar
100 g/4 oz self-raising flour
paper cake cases

To decorate
75 g/3 oz butter
175 g/6 oz icing sugar
lemon curd

Melt the butter in a saucepan. Remove from the heat and add the egg, milk and sugar. Mix well, then add the flour. Stand the paper cake cases in bun tins and divide the mixture between them. Cook in a moderate oven (180°C, 350°F, gas 4) for 20–25 minutes, until firm to the touch. Cool, in the cases, on a wire rack. Beat the butter and icing sugar together. Put into a piping bag fitted with a small star nozzle. Pipe a circle round the edge of each cake. Fill the centres with a teaspoonful of lemon curd.

ARTIST PARTY

What wonderful fun this is for children aged between five and eight, who love to be creative without worrying about making a mess! It does require you to be well-prepared, and assistance is definitely required, as some children will need encouragement and cleaning-up at the end.

The invitations can be shaped like an artist's palette with blobs of colour around the edge, and a thumbhole. Remember to tell the mums what sort of party it is, so they send the children dressed appropriately, or with an old shirt or apron to cover them up.

Keep the party mainly in the kitchen, although if the weather is good you could move the party outside. If you have, or can buy, some oddments of wallpaper, pin them on the walls in the kitchen, plain side out. Provide coloured chalks to use on them.

Cover the table with a plastic cloth and use as a printing area. Make sure you have a good supply of paper as budding artists need plenty. Buy some thin sponges, the sort you normally use for washing-up. Cut them into 5-cm/2-inch circles and soak in paint. Place them in a bun tin–this helps prevent paint spills. The best paint to use is powder paint mixed with water. It goes a long way and gives good strong colours. Have a choice of colours and have ready some potatoes, halved and cut into a design, cotton reels, leaves, pieces of sponge, slices of cardboard tube, anything that will make a mark of its own. You should have enough room for six children to do this without too much trouble. All they have to do is press the stamp into the sponge and make a pattern on their paper.

You might like to have paper and sticky tape ready so the children can make hats for themselves. Provide glue and different decorations to stick onto the hats, such as cotton wool, paper doilies, shiny wrappers from sweets, milk bottle tops, or even pasta! This mad burst of activity should end with helping hands clearing the tables for tea. After eating, there may be time for a couple of games, such as the following.

JIGSAW

Before the party, flip through some magazines and pull out some colourful pages, allowing about three per child. Cut each in half. Stick one half somewhere around the house, on a window, kitchen cupboard etc, somewhere that won't be damaged by sticky tape. Each child has half a picture and has to find the matching piece. They remove the other half and return it to you. You give them another one to match, and this goes on until you have had enough—or run out of pages!

MUSICAL SKETCH PADS

Space out sheets of newspaper on the ground, with one less than the number of children. Start the music. When the music stops each child must leap onto a piece of paper, and the child who does not find one is out. Remove another piece and start again until there is only one person left. This game can also be played in pairs; two people leaping for one piece of paper and trying not to fall off, causes lots of laughter!

PAINT-BY-NUMBERS

1 18 × 28 × 4-cm/7 × 11 × 1½-inch cake, use size two cake mix (see page 6)
4 tablespoons apricot jam, warmed
1 quantity decoration icing
1 paintbrush and food colouring

Bake the cake for 25–30 minutes. Turn out the cake onto a board. Spread it with the jam. Roll out the decoration icing and use it to cover the entire cake.

Leave it to dry. Using a fine paintbrush, draw a pattern and the message of your choice. Number each area according to colour. Fill in some areas to resemble paint-by-numbers. Leave a paint-brush on the top to decorate.

TECHNICOLOUR CAKES
Makes 24

175 g/6 oz soft margarine
175 g/6 oz caster sugar
3 eggs
175 g/6 oz self-raising flour
1 tablespoon cocoa powder
1 tablespoon water
pink and green food colourings
paper cake cases
2 tablespoons icing sugar
12 lollies

Beat the margarine, sugar, eggs and flour together for 2 to 3 minutes until smooth. Divide the mixture into three separate bowls. Mix the cocoa with the water and add to one bowl, a few drops of pink colouring to the second and green colouring to the third. Stand the paper cake cases in bun tins and put half a teaspoonful of each mixture into each case. Cook in a moderately hot oven (190°C, 375°F, gas 5) for about 20 minutes until golden-brown and firm to the touch. Remove from oven and cool, out of their cases, on a wire rack. Sprinkle with icing sugar. Stand a lolly in the top of each.

CHEESE PAINTBRUSHES
Makes about 24

Add a splash of colour to these jolly, edible paint-brushes with egg-yolk paints.

175 g/6 oz plain flour
pinch of salt
75 g/3 oz butter
75 g/3 oz cheese, grated
1 egg
2 egg yolks
yellow and green edible food colourings

Sift the flour and salt into a bowl and then rub in the butter. Add the cheese and bind the mixture with the egg. Roll out on a floured surface and cut into 1-cm/½-inch strips about 10-cm/4-inches long. Knead the trimmings back together and roll out again. Repeat the process until all the dough has been used. Place the strips onto greased baking sheets about 5-mm/¼-inch apart and make parallel cuts in one end for 'bristles'. Put each egg yolk into a small bowl. Mix yellow colouring into one yolk, green colouring into the other. Using a pastry brush, brush a little egg yolk paint onto the 'bristles', painting some yellow, some green. Cook in a moderately hot oven (190°C, 375°F, gas 5) for 10–15 minutes until golden. Cool on a wire rack.

PAINT-BOX JELLY
Serves 12 (Fills 4 ice-cube trays)

Borrow extra ice-cube trays from friends and neighbours to create this special effect!

1 packet raspberry jelly
1 packet pineapple jelly
1 packet lime jelly
212-g/7½-oz can red cherries
230-g/8½-oz can pineapple rings
small bunch (about 225 g/8 oz) seedless white grapes

Make up the jellies according to the directions on the packet. Drain the cherries and remove any stones. Put one or two cherries in each section of one row of a divided ice-cube tray and fill up with red jelly. Repeat the process with pieces of pineapple and yellow jelly, grapes and lime jelly. Chill the jellies until set. Dip the trays briefly in hot water to loosen the jelly and remove the dividers. Serve the assorted jelly cubes, from the trays, with ice-cream.

PAINT-POT PUFFS
Makes 36

370-g/13-oz packet frozen puff pastry, thawed
3 tablespoons icing sugar
3 tablespoons red jam
3 tablespoons lemon curd
3 tablespoons blackcurrant jam
3 tablespoons apricot jam

Roll out the pastry on a lightly floured surface, until 5-mm/¼-inch thick. Stamp out 5-cm/2-inch rounds with a pastry cutter. Place on dampened baking trays. Press a slightly smaller cutter (or use a bottle top) into the centre of each, taking care not to cut right through. Cook in a preheated hot oven (220°C, 425°F, gas 7) for 10–15 minutes until risen and golden. Transfer to a wire rack. Push the centres in with your thumb, and leave to cool. Sift icing sugar over the cases. Slightly warm each jam in the pot in a bowl of hot water before spooning it into the cases with a teaspoon. Arrange the cases.

CRUNCHY DIPPERS
Serves 12

Good hot or cold, and children love the familiar dip.

450 g/1 lb skinless pork sausages
3 tablespoons plain flour
2 eggs
100 g/4 oz fresh breadcrumbs
oil for frying
12 fish fingers
200-g/7.05-oz jar sandwich spread
6 tablespoons natural yogurt

Cut the sausages in half, and coat lightly with the flour. Beat the eggs in a wide shallow bowl with 2 tablespoons water. Spread the crumbs in another bowl. Dip the sausages into the egg, then crumbs, turning them until completely coated. Heat about 2.5-cm/1-inch of oil in a deep frying pan. Cook the sausages a few at a time for about 8 minutes, turning occasionally, until crisp and golden. Drain on kitchen paper. Grill or fry the fish fingers according to directions on packet. Drain on kitchen paper. Cut each one into three. Spear sausages and fish fingers with cocktail sticks. Dilute the sandwich spread with the yogurt and put into a bowl. Arrange the sausages and fish fingers around the dip and let the children help themselves.

PREHISTORIC PARTY

This party will be appreciated most by eight to twelve year olds who have learned about this period of history at school. There's not much to prepare for the games but it would be an advantage to have a bit of space, preferably outside, as some of the games involve chasing around. Older children like active parties but to prevent them getting over-excited and argumentative, it's best to alternate noisy and quieter games!

There are several alternatives for invitations, cut out a dinosaur shape, or more simply draw a dinosaur peeping round the edge of the card. He could then be speaking—put the details in a bubble coming from his mouth. A piece of grey card could be made to look like a stone slab with the information plus a few "UGS" and "ERGS" written on it. If you'd like people to reply, then it is best to put an extra section on the bottom for them to cut off and return.

Dressing-up can make this party even more fun, but it is not essential. The children will enjoy being 'dragged' in by the hair and occasionally coshed with a papier-maché club! The prehistoric nosh includes dinosaur ribs and chicken wings plus lots of other theme food to satisfy the heartiest stone-age appetites!

Start the party with a game that latecomers can easily join in, like Hunt the Stewpan.

LAME WOLF

You need a small area that is 'home' for the wolf and another that is 'home' for the lambs. One child is the wolf, he stands in his 'home'. The other children are lambs and they have to run around the wolf shouting "Lame wolf! lame wolf". Suddenly the wolf must chase after the lambs, but he can only take three steps before he has to hop after them. The lambs have to run for the shelter of the 'home' but any caught are either out, also become wolves, or can take the place of the wolf.

CRANES AND CROWS

This game is definitely best played outside. The children split into a team of crows and a team of cranes, one on either side of the garden. You stand in the middle and they start walking towards you while you say "Crrrrrrrr . . .". Suddenly you shout either "Crows!" or "Cranes!". The team you call must try and catch the other team before they can run back to base. Any children caught swap to the other side and the game continues until the whole of one team has been caught.

PTERODACTYL RACE

Draw six pterodactyls (they don't have to be exact to scale drawings, just a general idea. This may involve a visit to the library!) on stiff card. Make them about 30-cm/12-inch long. Attach equal lengths of string (about 3-metres/9-feet) to their heads. Tie the other end to a pencil and fix in place with sticky tape. Six children sit in a row, someone says "Go", and they all roll their pencils round furiously to pull the dinosaur towards them. The first pterodactyl to touch the pencil is the winner.

HUNT THE STEWPAN

All you need is a saucepan and a long wooden spoon. One child is blindfolded and kneels down on the floor. The saucepan is put somewhere in front of them and they have to find it by waving the spoon about and tapping the ground in front, until they eventually hit the pan. Then someone else has a turn. The other children help by shouting instructions.

ICE-AGE CAKE

**1 2 litre tub Neopolitan ice cream (choose one
  with distinctly separate sections)**
300 ml/½ pint whipping cream
candles and candleholders
prehistoric monster toys

Line the base of a 20-cm/8-inch diameter spring-form tin with greaseproof paper. Carefully spoon chocolate ice-cream from the tub into the tin. Working quickly, spread it over base and sides. Return it to the freezer until it hardens. Spread a layer of pink ice-cream into the tin and freeze. Finish with a layer of vanilla ice-cream. Freeze until required. Run a knife round the edge of the tin and turn out the ice-cream onto a chilled plate.

Whip the cream until it just forms soft peaks. Spread it over the top of the cake, allowing it to trickle down the sides. Add candles and a friendly dinosaur!

CAVE-MAN CLUBS
Makes 24

Children will enjoy chewing on these home-made bread sticks.

283-g/10-oz packet brown bread mix
1 tablespoon black poppy seeds
1 tablespoon sesame seeds

Make up the bread mix with warm water according to the directions on the packet. Divide the dough into 24 pieces. Knead each piece until smooth and make into a sausage shape. Roll one end under the palm of your hand to make it longer and thinner at that end. Arrange on greased baking trays, leaving space between them for rising. Cover tray with oiled cling film and leave in a warm place for about 30 minutes or until doubled in size. Remove cling film. Brush 'clubs' with beaten egg. Sprinkle poppy seeds over the thick ends of one half and sesame seeds over the thick ends of the rest. Bake in a hot oven (220°C, 425°F, gas 7) for about 15 minutes until crisp and golden. Cool on a wire rack.

DINOSAUR RIBS
Serves 12

Even small cave men and women like to chew on bones!

**About 1.4 kg/3 lb pork spare ribs (allow two
  per child)**
2 tablespoons oil
1 large onion, chopped
1 clove garlic, skinned and crushed (optional)
2 tablespoons tomato purée
4 tablespoons vinegar
3 tablespoons clear honey
1 beef stock cube

Separate the ribs with a sharp knife. Place them in a roasting tin and cook in a moderately hot oven (190°C, 375°F, gas 5) for 30 minutes. Meanwhile, make the sauce. Heat the oil in a saucepan, fry the onion and garlic for 3 minutes. Add the tomato purée, vinegar, honey and stock cube, dissolved in 150 ml/¼ pint water. Let the mixture bubble for 10 minutes then brush onto the ribs. Cook for a further 45 minutes to 1 hour, turning once during cooking. Arrange on a plate lined with Chinese leaves to serve.

CHICKEN WINGS WITH PEANUT SAUCE
Serves 12

These are cheap when bought in freezer packs, and again such fun to eat with fingers. You could also use chicken drumsticks.

12 chicken wings (thawed if frozen)
150 ml/¼ pint natural yogurt
1 tablespoon oil
1 small onion, finely chopped
4 tablespoons crunchy peanut butter
2 teaspoons lemon juice
150 ml/¼ pint water

Prick chicken wings in several places with a fine skewer. Put in a bowl with the yogurt, season, and stir until coated. Leave to marinate for two hours. Heat the oil in a saucepan, add onion and fry until transparent. Add the peanut butter, lemon juice and water and bring to the boil stirring. Allow to cool. Lift chicken wings out of marinade and place in a large roasting tin. Add marinade to peanut sauce then brush over the chicken. Cook in a moderately hot oven (190°C, 375°F, gas 5) for 30 minutes until juices run clear when the thickest part of the meat is pierced. Serve hot or cold.

FRUIT SPEARS
Makes 12

Vary the fruit according to the season, using stawberries, melon, and peach or nectarine slices in the summer.

3 bananas
2 tablespoons lemon juice
350 g/12 oz seedless grapes
455-g/15-oz can of pineapple cubes in juice
411-g/14½-oz can of apricot halves
2 tablespoons lemon juice

Peel the bananas and toss in the lemon juice to prevent browning. Wash and dry the grapes. Drain the pineapple cubes and apricot halves. Thread the fruits alternately onto 12 thin plastic drinking straws (safer than metal skewers). You may need to pierce a hole through the fruit with a skewer first.

CHOC ROCKS
Makes 24

These are simply choux buns filled with whipped fresh cream and topped with chocolate sauce.

Choux Pastry
75 g/3 oz butter
225 ml/8 fl oz water
100 g/4 oz plain flour, sifted
3 eggs, lightly beaten
300 ml/½ pint whipping cream

Chocolate Sauce
100 g/4 oz plain dessert chocolate
25 g/1 oz butter
2 tablespoons milk
½ teaspoon vanilla essence

To make the pastry, melt the butter in the water in a large pan. Bring to the boil, remove from heat and immediately tip in all the flour. Beat with a wooden spoon until the paste is smooth and forms a ball in the pan. Allow to cool slightly, then beat in the eggs a little at a time. (Use an electric mixer if you like.) Beat hard, until the paste is smooth and shiny. Using two teaspoons, place 24 walnut-sized blobs of pastry onto greased baking trays, leaving space between them to allow for rising. Bake in a preheated hot oven (220°C, 425°F, gas 7) for 15–20 minutes until crisp and golden. Transfer to a wire rack and cut a slit in the side of each bun. Leave to cool completely. Whip the cream and pipe or spoon it inside the choux buns. To make the chocolate sauce, melt the chocolate and butter in a bowl over a saucepan of hot water. Stir in milk and vanilla essence. Spoon a little sauce over the top of each bun and arrange them on a serving plate.

FIREWORKS PARTY

This is not necessarily a suggestion for a birthday party because Fireworks Day is so exciting that it's always a good excuse for a get-together. This party will probably be held in the evening so there may be adults to consider too. This is the sort of party that a group of parents might hold together, so they can pool resources. If you plan to go to a public firework display, you can enjoy the food before or after going out. Everyone knows how dangerous fireworks can be, and the rules for handling or storing them. We are not going to list a lot of warnings here as we are assuming you will have considered all these aspects before embarking on the party.

Start saving cardboard tubes from loo rolls or kitchen foil before the party, to make the invitations. Cut 10 cm/4 inch tubes, then wrap them in some snazzy paper, or paint them. Write the information on a sticky label and stick onto the tube. Stuff the inside of the tube with crumpled blue tissue paper and twist the top to look like the blue touch paper.

It is difficult to play games outside in the dark and if you are having a display you won't need games anyway. On the other hand, if you are having an indoor party, and no display, then a few ideas have been suggested here. As it is very near Halloween, combine the two occasions by decorating the house with lanterns made from hollow pumpkins or swedes. Have silver foil moons and stars or tinsel round the house, with black paper silhouettes of witches on broom-sticks stuck to the windows. If you are having the party outside, put night-lights in jam-jars so they don't blow out. For a real treat, organise a sing-song or story-telling around a bonfire.

Plenty of piping hot, filling food is essential to keep guests warm and happy. Grown-ups will like our suggestions too, but, remember they'll eat bigger portions!

MASK MAKING

Cut out the shapes for very young children, older ones will prefer to cut out their own mask. Use thickish paper in different colours, and have bright-coloured paints, chalks, sticky shapes, glitter, cotton wool, coloured wools, bits of trimmings and plenty of glue. Let the children decorate their own masks after you have cut the eyeholes in the right place. Have some fine elastic ready for stapling on each side of the mask.

BALLOON HEADS

When the children arrive, they could help decorate by drawing faces on balloons with felt pens, then hang the balloons around the room. Have some balloons already prepared and let the children take their own creations home when they leave.

ROUND-THE-BONFIRE GAMES

WITCHES' BREW

One person starts a story. "Once there was an ugly witch who made a spell. Into her cauldron she put an . . . - - - - (some item beginning with the letter A)". The next person must repeat the story so far and add an item beginning with B and so on around the circle until you reach Z. It gets more difficult as the list gets longer.

THIS IS MY KNEE

One person says "this is my knee Mary," while pointing to a totally different part of his body, ie. his nose. The person this remark is addressed to must touch the named part (on their own body!) but claim "this is my elbow (or some other part of the anatomy) Fred." And so it goes on. Anyone who makes a mistake, or a repetition is out.

FISTFUL OF SPARKLERS

2 large Swiss rolls, about 20-cm/8-inches long
2 quantities butter icing
red, pink and green food colourings
½ quantity decoration icing
1 packet indoor sparklers

Place one Swiss roll on a cake board, leaving space at one end for the 'hand'. Colour one quantity butter icing red and spread over the Swiss roll. Make the icing thicker at one end to represent the cuff. Run the tines of a fork along the icing in rows to resemble wool. Cut an 11-cm/4½-inch length off the other Swiss roll. Stand it upright at the 'cuff' end of 'sleeve'. Cut the remainder in half lengthways. Stick the pieces around two sides of the upright piece with butter icing, to make the hand shape. Colour the decoration icing pink and roll out four long sausage shapes to make fingers. Make one sausage shape a bit shorter and fatter for thumb. Position them on the cake. Colour the rest of the butter icing green and, using a small star nozzle, pipe in lines on the 'hand' to resemble a woolly fingerless glove. Push the sparklers into the sponge inside the hand.

JUMPING JACKS
Makes 24

370-g/13-oz packet frozen puff pastry, thawed
100 g/4 oz smooth spreading pâté
1 tablespoon tomato purée

Cut the pastry in half. Roll out each half into a 23 × 25.5-cm/9 × 10-inches rectangle. Beat the pâté and tomato purée together and spread thinly over the two pastry rectangles. Fold long end of pastry in about 4-cm/1½-inch, then fold under. Repeat folding over and under, like folding a fan, so the final shape resembles a jumping jack. Repeat with other pastry rectangle. Cut each into 12 slices. Place flat on baking trays, allowing space for rising. Press down lightly

and cook in a preheated moderately hot oven (220°C, 425°C, gas 7) for about 12 minutes until crisp and golden. Serve warm.

OATY BISCUITS
Makes 36

100 g/4 oz margarine
100 g/4 oz granulated sugar
1 tablespoon honey
100 g/4 oz self-raising flour
100 g/4 oz rolled oats
½ teaspoon bicarbonate of soda
1 teaspoon ground ginger

Melt the margarine, sugar and honey in a saucepan, stirring occasionally. Add the flour, oats, bicarbonate of soda and ginger and mix well. Use two teaspoons to shape small balls and place, spaced well apart, on greased baking trays. Cook in a moderate oven (180°C, 350°F, gas 4) for 15 minutes. Allow to cool on the tray for 2–3 minutes before transferring to a wire rack.

BREAD PUDDING
Serves 12

450 g/1 lb brown bread
600 ml/1 pint milk
350 g/12 oz mixed sultanas and raisins
100 g/4 oz dried apricots, quartered
100 g/4 oz shredded suet
100 g/4 oz soft brown sugar
1 tablespoon ground mixed spice
2 eggs, beaten
3 tablespoons demerara sugar

Cut the crusts off the bread. Break it into small pieces and place in a large bowl. Pour the milk over it and leave to soak for 30 minutes. Squeeze out the bread and beat with a wooden spoon to break up the lumps. Add the dried fruit, apricots, suet, sugar and spice. Mix well. Add the eggs and a little extra milk, if necessary, to give a dropping consistency. Pour mixture into a greased and greaseproof-lined 1.8-litre/3-pint roasting tin. Sprinkle demerara sugar over the top and cook in a moderate oven (180°C, 350°F, gas 4) for 1½ hours until firm. Leave to cool before removing from tin and cutting into pieces.

WELSH RAREBIT SLICES
Serves 12

You can replace the pickle, if you prefer, with a slice of ham, lightly fried onion or mushrooms or even canned pineapple.

50 g/2 oz butter
6 tablespoons milk
350 g/12 oz grated Cheddar cheese
½ teaspoon dry mustard
24 slices of French bread
6 tablespoons sweet pickle

Put the butter, milk, cheese and mustard into a saucepan and heat gently, stirring, until smooth and creamy. Toast the bread on one side only. Spread a little pickle over the untoasted side of the bread slices. Spread the cheese mixture over to cover the bread completely. Grill until bubbling and golden.

WHIZZ-BANG SOUP
Serves 12

2 800-g/1.7-lb cans cream of tomato soup
4 frankfurters
100 g/4 oz grated cheese

Heat the soup in a large pan, stirring occasionally. Do not allow to boil. Slice frankfurters thinly. Just before serving, add frankfurters and grated cheese to the soup and stir until the cheese melts. Serve in mugs.

MINI-TOADS
Makes 24

100 g/4 oz plain flour
pinch salt
1 egg
300 ml/½ pint milk
oil
12 pork or beef chipolatas

Preheat oven to hot (220°C, 425°F, gas 7). Sift the flour and salt into a bowl and make a well in the centre. Break the egg into the well and add a little milk. Mix with a fork, gradually incorporating the flour, until you have a smooth paste. Gradually add the rest of the milk, beating well after each addition. Pour into a jug. Put a few drops of oil and half a sausage in each well of two 12-hole bun tins and heat in the oven for 5 minutes. Quickly pour batter into the bun tins and return tins to the oven. Cook for about 20 minutes until well-risen and golden.

JACKET POTATOES
Serves 12

Speed up the cooking in a conventional oven by threading the potatoes on metal skewers. This conducts the heat right to the centre. Of course, if you have a microwave oven, you can simply pop the potatoes in it, resting them on paper towels, and they will cook in only 6-8 minutes, per potato, on the highest setting.

12 medium potatoes
oil
butter

Scrub potatoes well. Put into a pan of cold water and bring to the boil. Drain well, then rub skins with oil. Put on a baking tray and cook in a moderately hot oven (200°C, 400°F, gas 6) for 1-1¼ hours, until tender when pierced with a skewer. Make a deep cross cut in each potato. Squeeze each potato gently at the cross to open it out. Top with a knob of butter.

CHRISTMAS BIRTHDAY PARTY

At this time of year, there is so much going on that it can be hard to find the time or energy, let alone the money, to have a children's party. But it is lovely for a child to celebrate his birthday with his friends. Christmas-born children can sometimes miss out, but this year let our plan help you to make the day. Some elements that are obviously part of Christmas will add to the party feel, such as the decorations, the tree, and the prospect of breaking up from school. You must make sure that invitations are given out in plenty of time so other parents can include the party in their plans. One idea for invitations is to send a Christmas card but with the party details inside instead of the usual Christmas greeting. Or, make some biscuits in a Christmas tree or star shape, but cut a hole right through before baking. Tie a present label with the party details on it through the hole.

The food we suggest is about as far away as you can get from the usual traditional fare. There will be, or has been, plenty of that. The cake, however, has a Christmas theme, a Christmas tree with a sparkling, festive finish.

CHRISTMAS TREASURE HUNT

Gather together twelve smallish items such as a button, a crayon, a cotton reel, clothes peg, building block etc. Hide them around the house, perhaps sew the button on the curtain, clip the peg on a cushion, but remember to keep things at a child's eye level. Give the children a list of items. They have to remember where they saw all the different things and go and search for them. The first one to tell you where everything is wins.

SOCK FUMBLING

Take a large, thick woolly sock and put one item in the bottom of it without the children seeing it. Each child comes to you in turn to feel the sock and whisper to you what is inside. Have a mixture of items, some more unusual and puzzling things. For instance, a grape, a sprout, a marble, a sachet of shampoo, a sponge, spoon, crayon or domino.

SANTA'S SUPPER

Sit the children in a circle with one of them in the middle, blindfolded. Put a mince pie on a plate or a packet of sweets behind him. Point to one of the children sitting in the circle. They must get up and tiptoe round the outside of the circle, back through their space and behind the central person to pick up the mince pie. As they creep round, the person in the middle must listen and try to point to them. If he or she points to them correctly they change places. Any "creeper" that reaches the pie or sweets wins them.

SNOWFLAKES

Have ready lots of pieces of paper folded into quarters. You will also need several pairs of scissors, crayons and felt-tip pens. Get the children to cut out patterns so that when they open up the paper they have a cut-out snowflake, which they can colour in and take home. This is a good activity for the end of the party just before the children go home.

OUTDOOR GAMES

If there is snow on the ground and the children are well wrapped they can get together and build the biggest/smallest/fattest snowman ever! And every-

one enjoys a snowball fight – until they get snow down the back of the neck! Small children get cold very quickly so don't keep them outdoors too long.

CHRISTMAS TREE

1 21.5 × 29 × 5-cm/8½ × 11½ × 2-inch chocolate cake, use size three cake mix (see page 6)
1 quantity butter icing
green food colouring
foil-wrapped chocolate balls
coloured and silver balls
a few small crackers
tinsel

Bake the cake for 30–35 minutes. Colour the butter icing green and spread over the top of the cake. Cut eight 6-cm/2½-inch squares from the cake. Cut each square in half diagonally to make sixteen triangles. Arrange in rows as shown in the picture, on a large cakeboard, to make a Christmas tree shape. Use a piece of the remaining cake to make the 'trunk'. Put a foil-wrapped chocolate on each triangle and add the silver and coloured balls and the crackers. Put a piece of tinsel round the trunk.

SAMOSAS
Makes 12

Lots of children like slightly spicy food, but if yours don't, use 2 tablespoons tomato purée instead of the curry.

Filling
1 tablespoon oil
1 medium-sized onion, finely chopped
225 g/8 oz minced beef
1 teaspoon mild curry powder or curry paste

Pastry
225 g/8 oz plain flour
½ teaspoon salt
50 g/2 oz butter
2 to 4 tablespoons warm milk
oil for deep-frying

To make the filling, heat the oil in a saucepan and fry the onion until transparent. Add the beef and curry powder and fry, stirring until browned. Cook gently, stirring occasionally for 10 minutes. Allow to cool. To make the pastry, sift the flour and salt into a bowl. Melt the butter and stir into the flour. Gradually add enough milk to make a soft, pliable dough. Roll out dough and use a pastry cutter to stamp out twelve 10-cm/4-inch circles. Put one spoonful of the filling in the centre of each circle. Brush the edges with water and fold the circle in half, pinching the edges together. Heat the oil in a deep-frying pan to 180°C, 350°F and fry the samosas a few at a time for about 3 minutes, turning once. When golden-brown, remove from pan and drain on kitchen paper. Serve immediately, or cool and reheat later. Place on a baking tray and heat in a moderate oven (180°C, 350°F, gas 4) for 10–15 minutes before serving with Cucumber and Yogurt Dip.

CUCUMBER AND YOGURT DIP

½ cucumber
300 ml/½ pint natural yogurt
1 tablespoon mango chutney or apricot jam

Peel the cucumber and chop it very finely. Mix into the yogurt with the mango chutney or apricot jam. Serve as a dip with the Samosas.

SAUSAGE KEBABS
Makes 12

These tasty skewerfuls will disappear quickly. Don't forget the ketchup though!

675 g/1½ lb pork or beef chipolatas
450 g/1 lb rindless streaky bacon rashers
6 thick slices of bread
100 g/4 oz butter, melted
4 tomatoes

Cut the sausages in half and wrap each piece in half a bacon rasher. Cut the bread into 2.5-cm/1-inch cubes and dip into the melted butter. Thread the sausages and bread cubes alternately onto skewers and cook in a moderately hot oven (200°C, 400°F, gas 6) for 20 minutes or until golden brown. Add a tomato wedge to each skewer. Serve warm with tomato ketchup.

PAVLOVA
Serves 12

A super party centrepiece. The addition of candles will transform it into the birthday cake.

4 egg whites
¼ teaspoon salt
225 g/8 oz caster sugar
4 teaspoons cornflour
2 teaspoons vinegar
½ teaspoon vanilla essence
300 ml/½ pint whipping cream
a selection of fresh or canned fruit

Whisk egg whites until they stand in stiff peaks. Continue to whisk while adding the sugar a tablespoon at a time. Whisk in the cornflour, vinegar and vanilla essence. Use the bottom of a large (about 25-cm/10-inch) cake tin or plate to draw a circle on a piece of non-stick baking paper. Line a baking tray with the paper and use the circle as a guide to spread the meringue mixture into a round. Bake in a cool oven (140°C, 275°F, gas 1) for about 1¼ hours. Allow to cool. Transfer to a large, flat serving plate. Whip the cream until stiff and spread over the Pavlova. Top with your chosen fruit.

HONEYED BARS
Makes 12

Shortbready biscuits with a knobbly topping.

175 g/6 oz plain flour
50 g/2 oz caster sugar
100 g/4 oz margarine
2 tablespoons clear honey
25 g/1 oz chopped nuts
50 g/2 oz chocolate chips

Sift the flour into a bowl and add the sugar and margarine. Rub in with the fingertips until the mixture resembles fine breadcrumbs. Knead the mixture together to form a firm, smooth dough. Press the shortbread into a greased 18 × 28-cm/7 × 11-inch Swiss roll tin. Mix the honey, nuts and chocolate chips together and spread over the top. Bake in a moderate oven (180°C, 350°F, gas 4) for 25 minutes. Cool in the tin for 5 minutes, then cut into 12 bars. Cool on a wire rack.

INDEX